# LEADER'S
# BLOCK

'In this book, Ritu has explored an aspect of leadership that we don't talk or hear about often. It is an honest recount of the leaders she interviewed and also her own corporate journey. The book is very engaging as it's peppered with interesting narratives and anecdotes. My favourite chapter is 'Leaders in Action'. I highly recommend this book to all leaders irrespective of their background and experience'—'Tiger' Tyagarajan, president and CEO, Genpact

'Ritu Mehrish has done something that is very rare in leadership literature: found a topic that is crucial for leaders to understand, yet one that we have not talked about at all, not even had a name for! I am convinced that 'leader's block' will become a common leadership phrase and the world will become a much better place because of it as companies, organizations and leaders learn to identify, diagnose and treat this phase. This is an important book that should be mandatory reading for managers at all levels'—Fredrik Haren, author of *The Idea Book*, included in the recently published book *The 100 Best Business Books of All Time*

'*Leader's Block* provides a lot of insights into the performance of business leaders. Ritu has done a great job in identifying a common problem that hinders business leaders from reaching their potential and making a significant impact. Leader's block is something many of us have experienced. What distinguishes Ritu's book is that not only does she identify it, she also provides concrete solutions for how managers, organizations and coaches can help address these blocks. Ritu leverages her own management experience as well as her executive coaching practice to bring many real cases to the table. This is a very great handbook for managers, coaches and HR professionals'—Wenjia Fang, South East Asia country manager, online publishing group, Google

'*Leader's Block* is a must-read for all. It reminds us of our own leader's block moments. It is assuring to know that this phase is transitionary. The book is exactly what the wellness coach ordered!'—Zarina Stanford, chief marketing officer (CMO), BackOffice Associates, former CMO (Asia–Pacific), SAP

'*Leader's Block* is inspiring and keeps the reader glued till the last page as it picks up on a taboo in our performance-driven business society. Ritu genuinely managed to get hundreds of leaders to talk about some of the most sensitive and vulnerable periods in their careers. Many of us will relate to the book in some form or the other. *Leader's Block* will help us reach meaningful objectives in the job, and in life, more sustainably'—Thomas Kessler, principal finance specialist, sustainable development and climate change department, Asian Development Bank

'I found myself recognizing situations that I had faced. Understanding the perspectives of others in similar situations provided great insight. Ritu's succinct style of bringing everything together further enhanced the experience'—Neville Ravji, president and CEO, Volterra Energy Holdings LLC

'Leader's Block is a simple yet elegant work that gives a name to a phenomenon that all leaders regularly suffer from. Through extensive first-hand research, filtered through her own experiences, Ritu Mehrish has made an important contribution to leadership literature with this book'—Vishal Sharma, partner, deal advisory, KPMG

'Ritu has explored a topic that is so prevalent and yet not talked about. The book is very relatable and talks to leaders at every level, providing helpful guidance in getting the best out of people at work. Highly recommendable!'—Sanjeev Narula, senior vice president, finance and business operations, Pfizer

# RITU G. MEHRISH

Foreword by Marshall Goldsmith

# LEADER'S BLOCK

## HOW GREAT LEADERS
## RECOVER AFTER THEY STUMBLE

PENGUIN
BUSINESS

An imprint of Penguin Random House

PORTFOLIO

USA | Canada | UK | Ireland | Australia
New Zealand | India | South Africa | China | Singapore

Portfolio is part of the Penguin Random House group of companies
whose addresses can be found at global.penguinrandomhouse.com

Published by Penguin Random House India Pvt. Ltd
4th Floor, Capital Tower 1, MG Road,
Gurugram 122 002, Haryana, India

Penguin
Random House
India

First published in Portfolio by Penguin Random House India 2019

Copyright © Ritu Gupta Mehrish 2019
Foreword copyright © Marshall Goldsmith 2019

Illustrations by Orlando J. Oliveros

ISBN 9780670091928

Typeset in Aldine401 BT by Manipal Digital Systems, Manipal

Printed at Replika Press Pvt. Ltd.

www.penguin.co.in

MIX
Paper from
responsible sources
FSC® C016779

*To Samar and Nandini*

# Contents

# Foreword

In my forty years of working as an executive educator and coach for top CEOs across the world, I have been instrumental in removing the stigma attached to coaching. I spearheaded the movement that was responsible for moving coaching from being negative to now, when leaders and organizations look at it as an investment. In a similar way, Ritu's work and approach to leader's block is about removing the stigma attached to it. She has given a name to a problem that is so common. Her work reflects her earnestness and passion for a topic that we don't feel comfortable talking about. She has taken a unique spin on leadership and presented a human side to it.

Almost all leaders go through a phase in their career where they feel demotivated, uninspired, lost and not on top of their game. This could be triggered by various internal and external reasons like lack of stimulation in their roles, misalignment of their goals versus the organization's goals, resistance to unlearn and relearn, personal factors, and so on. If this phase is not addressed, it has a negative impact on the leader, his or her team and the organization. An uninspired leader cannot inspire others. The purpose of this book is to give a name to this phase—leader's block—and to help leaders recognize and acknowledge these patterns, and work on overcoming this phase and preventing derailment and burnouts.

Ritu has over twenty years of experience of working across the globe. As a former business leader with Procter & Gamble, GE Capital and its spin-off, Genpact, she has worked with people in countries across five continents and experienced leadership from close quarters. She has been a leader and worked with some of the stalwarts in P&G and GE. In the last five years, her work as an executive coach and global speaker for some of the world's best-known organizations like Google, PayPal, J.P. Morgan, Applied Materials, Johnson & Johnson, Swiss Re and AIA has given her further insights into leadership. Working with leaders across a variety of industries, nationalities and age, she has found a common thread.

In *Leader's Block*, Ritu has distilled her experience of being a leader and an executive coach.

The book is a refreshing and unique angle of presenting the human side to leadership by talking about the challenges leaders face during their journey. It's an honest account of what leaders go through and it is heartening to see that they opened up to her and shared their setbacks, failures, trials and tribulations.

Among the direct benefits of reading this book are that it will help leaders and organizations give a name to a phase that everyone goes through, help them recognize and acknowledge the symptoms, understand its impact and learn strategies and practices to overcome it, and prevent it from recurring. The icing on the cake is the account of leaders that she has called 'leaders in action'. These stories are not about being heroic but about the challenges and dilemmas that we don't get to see and read about often.

My favourite part of the book, however, is her personal account of going through leader's block. Rarely do you see people being so honest about their failures and setbacks.

I am confident that the term 'leader's block' will soon become part of corporate jargon. This book will catapult Ritu to the position of a thought leader in the space of leadership with a new twist.

I am delighted to see that she has made references to some of my works like *What Got You Here Won't Get You There*, the stakeholder-centred coaching methodology and the philosophy and process of feedforward. I am glad that my work has been recommended as part of the solution to recognizing and overcoming leader's block.

I am also excited to take this concept and share it with the leaders and the MG100 coaches whom I coach. I am sure leaders at all levels—managers, senior leaders and CEOs—will benefit from this concept and find it very relatable. I would highly recommend that every leader read this book as they will find their own stories in it in some way or the other.

Last, but not the least, Ritu's approach ties in very well with my overall theme and motto of helping successful people achieve positive, lasting change and behaviours for themselves, their people and their teams.

Marshall Goldsmith
Leadership thinker, coach and educator, and bestselling author of *What Got You Here Won't Get You There*, *Triggers* and more

# Preface

As an executive coach, I have had the privilege of working with brilliant leaders across many regions and industries. As I listened and worked with them on their challenges it dawned on me that there are thousands of books, articles and motivational talks that tell leaders how to get better, how to be more effective, how to be more productive, how to be more profitable and how to be more successful. But, few talk about the challenges, fears and dilemmas that leaders experience.

In this book, I have given a name to their temporary challenges and dilemmas, and have shared insights on how to recognize, acknowledge, overcome and prevent this state of being in the future. I call it 'leader's block'.

This is a book written for leaders by leaders. The discernments and highlights here are based on intensive and in-depth interviews and conversations with more than 200 leaders across various geographies and industries, and my own twenty years in the corporate world. I have researched this topic extensively, studying articles, leadership books and research papers to find links, data and evidence to support or contradict leader's block. It is critically important that we, as leaders, have supporting evidence along with positive insights and recommendations to assess, understand and eliminate leader's block when it appears.

This book is especially relevant to human resource leaders and recruiters as it presents them with the personal insights of leaders and provides a perspective on how the organization can support them better in their journey. For CEOs, it will give an insight into the minds and lives of the leaders who helped them become great. CEOs, too, are not immune to leader's block!

As leaders shared their stories with me, I discovered a little bit of myself within each of them. I could relate to the stories and emotions that they spoke about, and my hope is that you too can find a little bit of yourself in these stories and anecdotes and learn how to deal with leader's block.

# 1

# What Is Leader's Block?

Is leadership an art or a science? There are enough arguments and explanations in support of both sides, and yet we have no winner. The science part comes from the processes such as systems thinking, appreciative inquiry and emotional intelligence, as well as tools such as MBTI (Myers–Briggs Type Indicator)[1] and Hogan Assessments.[2] The art part of leadership is based on the belief that leadership

---

[1]  MBTI: Myers–Briggs Type Indicator was developed by Isabel Briggs Myers and her mother, Katharine Briggs, to explain the theory of psychological types described by C.G. Jung.

[2]  Hogan Assessments are assessment tools that use personality scales and subscales to help leaders

is a mindset which requires thinking, acting in the moment and comes from who you are. Leadership is a state of being and doing, which come together to create results, and that's why each leader is so unique—just like an artist.

Over the last twenty-five years, I have had the opportunity to work with, coach and have conversations with leaders across the globe, all from diverse industries. During my journey, I have been surprised to see how these leaders have such different styles and personalities, and yet they have carved a place for themselves and are successful in their individual fields. Each leader is unique, and this led me to look at leadership as an art form and leaders as creative people.

In this book, I have taken a concept that has been associated with another set of creative people—writers—and applied it to leaders.

History has shown us that almost all great writers at some point in their career suffer from writer's block. According to Wikipedia, 'writer's block is a condition, primarily associated with writing, in which an author loses the ability to produce new work or experiences a creative slowdown. The condition ranges in difficulty from coming up with

---

recognize shortcomings, maximize strengths and build successful teams.

original ideas to being unable to produce a work for years'.

In the same way, leader's block is a condition in which a leader experiences a creative slowdown. In this state, leaders feel uninspired and demotivated and are unable to perform at their best. It is not uncommon that the leader may also experience low self-esteem, lack of focus, or an inability to make good decisions. Every leader is susceptible to leader's block. No leader in any field has ever had a consistent track record—sometimes they have led well, and at other times they have struggled.

Leader's block can be compared to being out of form in sports, which is used to describe a phase when a sportsperson is not able to perform to the best of his or her abilities. It's common in sports for players to be out of the team when they have an injury or if they are not playing their best. They take time out, they practice, recuperate and come back refreshed and recharged. It's an accepted normality in this space.

Almost all leadership books talk about how to be great leaders but not about the challenges and blocks that leaders face. This book talks about those challenges and blocks.

To find out more about leader's block and to test its existence and impact, I conducted in-depth, one-on-one interviews with more than a hundred leaders across industries and geographies. These were all leaders who had work experience of fifteen years or more. They came from a wide range of industries, from technology to banking to pharmaceuticals; from financial services to consumer goods; from the big giants to start-ups and non-profits.

Each of them had experienced leader's block in their career. Surprisingly, most leaders experience it after having worked for many years. When we are starting out in our career, there is usually a defined path and a process for us to do our job. If we get stuck, we reach out to our supervisors or peers for assistance. Early in our careers we are in an exploratory mode, we are trying to find our passion, so in case something doesn't work out, it's easier to change lanes as there is more flexibility.

As we gain seniority, the situations and scenarios we are faced with become complex. There is a lot of ambiguity that we deal with, such as the need to define processes and set the direction. But, it starts to get lonely. Sometimes, even that is unknown to us, till very late. The ego stops senior leaders from asking for help; they are not sure how they will be perceived so they start handling everything themselves.

After speaking to numerous leaders over the last two years, I am convinced that leader's block is something that happens to everyone. It's as common and pervasive as the flu. It may not be as frequent but everyone gets it at some point. It starts with a simple cough and the sniffles, which are self-healing in most cases. However, if the cough and cold continue for some time, they can lead to the flu. If you don't treat that, it can lead to pneumonia.

There are some early signs that signal the onset of leader's block, such as feeling demotivated or uninspired for a few days, or even a few weeks. If this situation is prolonged beyond a few weeks, it can quickly become leader's block, and this can last from a few months to a year—or longer! If leader's block is not treated, it can, and more often than not does, lead to burnout.

According to *Psychology Today*,[3] a burnout is not a simple outcome due to long working hours. The cynicism, depression and lethargy of a burnout can occur when you're not in control of how you carry out your job; when you're working toward goals that don't resonate with you; and when you lack social support. If you don't tailor your responsibilities to match your true calling, or at least take a break once in a while, you could face a mountain of mental and physical health problems.

---

[3] *Psychology Today* is a magazine published every two months in the United States of America since 1967.

Another parallel to leader's block is a road journey. Let me explain. During a road journey, we come across speed breakers and bumps on the road, which we overcome by slowing down. The road block that stops us from moving forward and forces us to change our direction is leader's block, and the dead end on this road is a burnout.

I have approached the topic of leader's block with the assumption that leaders start out with the right intentions. This book is both for and from them. There is no right or wrong, there is no judgement. This is an inside story of what leaders experience and it's a story of leaders like you and me, like the ones we work with. It's about leaders who have been successful in their fields, who have the right skills and the right will, but still find themselves blocked at some point.

As I look back at my own corporate journey of twenty years, one phase stands out for me.

It was November 2002. Our annual appraisal cycle had just been completed and the list of promotions was about to be issued. I was at an off-site training session when the list came out, and I discovered that my name wasn't on the list. I was very disappointed. After the training session, I took a day off to spend time at home (to brood). I went to office the next day with a brave face. But I don't think it worked. My manager called me to his office and asked me what was going on. I assumed that he was asking about how I was feeling. I told him that I was disappointed, but that it was okay. He didn't look convinced and asked me what was going on with my team. At this point, I was quite confused. I said that I didn't understand his question. Even as I write this, I still feel that overwhelming sense of pride, joy, surprise and shock that I felt after listening to what my manager told me. On the day that I was at the off-site training, my team had approached my manager to ask him why my name was not on the promotion list when I deserved it. They told him how they all shared in the disappointment and were unhappy about this outcome. My manager was taken aback. He had not seen this coming. It was the first time in his career that he had experienced something like that. He told them that they should trust the system and that it would only be a matter of time before I was promoted. This incident is one of the highlights of my career. I was still a young manager, but from that moment, I realized the strength of being a great leader. I was promoted after six months.

This experience has stayed with me throughout my career and has served me well.

Approximately five years later, and again at annual appraisal time, I was sitting in the office with my manager. He shared something with me that filled me with sadness. Two of my team members had complained to him that they were not happy with the quality of the discussions that I was having with them. I attempted to say something in my defence, but I knew that they were right. I had seen myself becoming disengaged in meetings; I was unusually quiet and distanced. I was not spending as much time with my team as I did before. We had not even gone for our monthly team dinners in the previous two months, which was considered sacrilege within our team. I walked out of my manager's office and thought to myself, *what's happened to me?* I am the same person whom the team stood up for five years earlier. Now there were complaints about me!

I had been doing the same role for the past five years and I was bored. I was on autopilot. There was nothing about the role that excited me or challenged me.

All my key performance metrics were green. I was delivering on my numbers. My client was happy.

But I was miserable.

Even though I had tried hard to hide it and not show my disengagement, it had manifested in ways I hadn't even realized—in this case, it had showed in the form of disinterest towards my team members. It was the lowest point in my professional career. I was in the middle of a classic leader's block! I was not performing my best, I was demotivated and uninspired.

I wonder why it is taboo for leaders to say that they are not at their best. Or is it that we don't talk openly about it as there is no name for this phase in our career as leaders? As humans, until we name or label something, we cannot address it. I hope that giving this phase a name—leader's block—will enable more open conversation about it.

There are several authors, professors and experts on leadership who have written about what makes leaders fail. Timothy Irwin in his book *Derailed*[4] talks about six CEOs and their downfall, the 'why' behind their failure and how they got derailed. 'Though expressed in a variety of behaviors', Irwin writes, 'they are all tied to a lack of failure of one of these four critical qualities: authenticity, self-management, humility, courage.'

Irwin has attributed the derailment of these character traits to the individual leaders. His book also talks about how you can detect these attitudes and behaviours in your own life.

One can argue that the CEOs in Irwin's book could have experienced leader's block, but they ignored it and found themselves derailed.

---

[4]   Timothy Irwin, *Derailed* (Thomas Nelson, 2009).

Comparably, in the article 'Off the Track: Why and How Successful Executives Get Derailed'[5] by Morgan McCall and the Center of Creative Leadership, the authors identify traits and behaviours associated with leaders who derail. They highlight how these leaders had strong technical skills, a string of prior successes and were viewed as being the highest potential leaders in their organizations. McCall says, 'While every leader had strengths and weaknesses, the research indicated six basic clusters of flaws in the leaders who derailed: problems with interpersonal relationships, difficulties selecting and building a team, difficulties in transitioning from the technical/tactical level to the general/strategic level, lack of follow-through, overdependence, strategic differences with management.'

Both these resources are very useful and an excellent read for all managers and leaders. Even though they were written over ten years ago, they are still relevant. Both provide an external perspective on leaders, their characteristics and the reasons why they derail and fail.

---

[5]  M. McCall and M. Lombardo, 'Off the Track: Why and How Successful Executives Get Derailed', (Technical Report, Center for Creative Leadership, No. 21) (Greensboro, NC: Center for Creative Leadership, 1983).

In this book, I try to bring an inside-out perspective on what leaders go through when they find themselves stalling due to external, and sometimes internal, circumstances. It is not necessarily caused by flaws in characters and behaviours. It is also worth noting that leader's block can be overcome without permanent damage to a leader's career and organization. The leader and organization are impacted, that is unavoidable, but it can be contained by overcoming the block in a timely fashion. Therefore, it is even more crucial to identify and recognize leader's block, which is a precursor to more drastic outcomes such as permanent derailment and burnouts.

In her book *Multipliers,*[6] Elizabeth Wiseman talks about multipliers and diminishers. Multipliers are genius-makers, people who make those around them smarter and more capable. Diminishers, on the other hand, make others feel stupid in their presence and think of themselves as the smartest people in the room. Wiseman shares an interesting insight about how all of us have an accidental diminisher within us. In fact, she has dedicated a chapter to narrating Bill Campbell's story about how he became a diminisher while he was working at previous organizations before leading at Intuit. Someone who has a reputation

---

[6] Elizabeth Wiseman, *Multipliers* (HarperBusiness, 2010).

for being a smart and successful leader, he would micromanage, not let go of control and shut people down in meetings. I would call this phase a diminisher leader's block. Bill managed to overcome it by getting candid feedback from his colleagues, which made him aware of his actions and allowed him to explore his conduct and why it was occurring. This is another case of experiencing and coming out of leader's block.

Dina Glouberman states in her book, *The Joy of Burnout:*[7] 'Burnout happens at work or at home when the meaning has gone out of what you are doing, but you have too much invested to stop and take notice. Your soul is whispering but you are not listening.' She describes it as a phase where you think you are at the point of no return.

*Reclaiming the Fire,*[8] by Steven Berglas, talks about a supernova burnout. 'The phenomenon I have studied for over twenty years is pervasive dissatisfaction with a successful career interrupted by often non-dramatic, yet incredibly debilitating, symptoms ranging from anxiety about living up to the expectations born of success to a sense of ennui born of the realization that

---

[7] Dr Dina Glouberman, *The Joy of Burnout* (Inner Ocean Publishing, 2003).

[8] Steven Berglas, *Reclaiming the Fire* (Random House, 2001).

attaining the goal you thought would change your life did no such thing,' the book says.

I am citing these examples and highlighting the definition of derailment and burnout because I want to draw a clear distinction between these phenomena and leader's block. However, leader's block can serve as a precursor to these outcomes if not addressed. One of the ways to prevent getting to that stage of derailment and burnout is to recognize, acknowledge and work on leader's block. I will discuss this further in later chapters. It is evident that if these leaders who had derailed caught themselves early, or if the signs had been identified by colleagues, then the situation could have been avoided.

A phrase that has gained popularity in recent times is 'getting into a funk'. It's an American phrase used to describe that slump, that emptiness we experience after completing a big task. Some have said it's not quite depression, but listlessness, purposelessness, an inability to motivate ourselves and a sense of caring about very little. This feeling is quite common for many after the year-end holidays. This could be an extended 'Monday morning blues' for others. A funk is a mood that is characterized by lack of motivation, grumpiness and general malaise. It could last a day to a week or even a few weeks. Based on multiple articles and discussions on social media, this is best overcome by doing things to distract our minds, such as taking a break from work or home, reading a book or watching a movie, connecting with people, waiting patiently for it to pass, exercising, or changing our routines.

We all get into a funk at some point. In some cases, if these fleeting feelings or moments continue for a long period of time, then one could be heading towards a leader's block.

In the flu analogy we used earlier, getting into a funk is like getting a cough and cold. It usually doesn't require any medication and you get over it on your own. However, if the cough and cold persist for more than the usual three to five days and seem to be getting worse, then remember—you could be heading towards the flu and it will need attention.

Leader's block is in between getting into a funk and a burnout.

To give a flavour of what leader's block may look like, let me share an excerpt from my conversation with Zoe. She is the chief marketing officer (CMO) for the Asia-Pacific region at a big technology and software company. I met her as part of my research for the book. We sat in her corner office on the thirty-second floor, overlooking the beautiful, landmark Marina Bay Sands hotel in Singapore. After thanking her for her time and exchanging the usual pleasantries,

I explained the meaning of leader's block to her and asked if she had ever experienced it. To my surprise, she replied, 'I'm actually thinking that I may be in that state right now and I'll tell you why I think that.' She said that she had begun to feel this way about a month, month and a half ago. She said that she was not able to achieve the results that she wanted to. She added, 'I run very fast and I've probably done this role at my previous organization a couple of times already, and so I don't have a lot of patience.' According to her, her team and the business were too slow for her, and it was frustrating as she found herself having to tell her team to do things that she had done five years ago. She went on to say, 'Yeah, so I think the current block I'm in is that I'm a little bit bored.' As she was speaking I could feel her dissatisfaction in her voice and body language. Sipping my coffee, I thought that to the outer world, Zoe's situation appeared perfect. She had a big role, a fancy title, a corner office, a big team to manage and a strategic agenda to drive. But in reality, she was bored. I went on to ask what was constraining her; she was a senior leader after all. Zoe smiled and said, 'That's a very good question and I ask myself that as well.' She thought it was a combination of external and internal factors. The internal factors were primarily related to her impatient personality. And the external was due to her environment. Zoe had joined her current organization about fifteen months back. She had come from another major technology company, which was very fast-paced. She seemed to be struggling with the calibre of the people at the current organization as it was very different from that of her previous one. The level of understanding and the level of openness, boldness and ability to take risks were on the opposite end of the spectrum.

I was curious to know how her journey in her current organization had been till then. She said that the first six months had been great; she was energized, excited and she got a lot of positive feedback and support for her ideas from the stakeholders, so it had all felt very good. But soon things began to change as she started interacting with her direct and extended teams.

She shared an example to illustrate her point. She and her team would brainstorm on a new marketing idea and the team would agree with it, but they would fail to execute. Some blamed it on not having enough resources, but Zoe felt it was because they didn't believe that it could be done. They lacked conviction. But being a leader, she pushed along. When Zoe wanted to get something done, she got it done. It built momentum, gave her more adrenaline, got her excited. For her, that was how success bred success.

Zoe was disgruntled, she was struggling with a tussle internally. She gave a vivid description of her state: 'I want to be sailing, but I feel like I have to pull the boat.' She was quick to add that as a leader she should be the one to figure out how to get out of the turbulent water.

I wasn't sure what was holding Zoe back. I asked her what actions she saw herself taking. She said that if she had her way, she would begin by changing two people in her team because they were not the right fit. After pausing for a few seconds, she said that from her standpoint, the speed of execution, innovation and adoption of technology was slow across the organization. But she didn't know exactly how long and what it would take to overcome the challenges. She continued, 'So now I'm at a juncture of saying do I want to keep pulling, as in be very determined, or do I recognize that I'm hitting a wall.'

We will find out later if Zoe managed to break through the leader's block and, if she did, what steps she took to overcome it.

Zoe's leader's block is an archetypal case, with senior leaders managing external environments and internal expectations. Zoe could not drive the results and get the outcomes that she wanted, as her environment was not able to support her vision. Lack of execution by her team and the slow pace of the organization were slowing her also down, leading to boredom and restlessness. It was a painful phase for her, as she felt restricted, stifled and unable to perform her best.

If leader's block is a common occurrence and has always existed, why is it that we are only talking about it now? In the past, people would remain in the same job for decades as they wanted the stability that big organizations provided. Since trends didn't change quickly, leader's block didn't have much of an impact on an individual or the company as a whole. As we all know, today's scenario is very different as there are changes and disruptions almost every day. Neither the organization nor the leader has the luxury to stay blocked. Today, innovation moves at breakneck speed. New companies are rising every day to squash the status quo and uninspired leaders and organizations simply cannot survive. The world demands more from leaders today than it ever did before. Besides the leaders' day jobs, they are expected to stay on top of current trends, embrace and lead change, make tough decisions, inspire others and much, much more. But what happens if the leader is blocked?

My dear friend Fredrik described it very well. He said that if you are driving a car on a US expressway in autopilot mode, you could doze off for a mile and nothing may happen to you—that was the scenario for leaders in the past. However, you can't take your eyes off the road if there are sharp turns every 100 metres—and that is the scenario today.

It's real and there is no escaping it; the key is to recognize and acknowledge it. During the course of my research for this book, I spoke to leaders across regions and industries, and they all said the same thing: they were relieved to know that they were not alone. To know that every leader goes through leader's block provided them with a sense of normality. It reassured them that there was nothing wrong with them. Keep in mind that leaders can get quite lonely and to some extent insecure. They don't open up very easily; they don't talk about their struggles and challenges openly. Having one universally accepted word or phrase to address this phenomenon is the first step towards acknowledging the block.

Imagine if organizations were able to address the leader's block in the early stages. If they could recognize it and acknowledge it, they would benefit immensely from the potential of having better leaders, leaders who are more effective and performing their best. Therefore, organizations also have a big role to play in supporting leaders to overcome the leader's block. We will talk more about this in later chapters.

All human resources (HR) leaders should know about the leader's block so that they understand when some of their best leaders go through a temporary dip in performance. Leader's block doesn't impact only the leaders who are going through it; it also impacts the organization, and therefore it's imperative for HR leaders and organizations to identify it, address it and help prevent it.

Leader's block is not a taboo! It's not about falling; it's about getting up again. The great leaders figure out how not to stay in it for long; they recognize it, acknowledge it and overcome it. If you haven't gone through it yet, you could be missing out on the clarity and wisdom that you gain when you overcome the block. Embrace it and leverage it to enhance your leadership effectiveness and your life.

Leader's block is a precursor to a burnout. It's not a stigma as everyone goes through it at some point in their careers.

# 2

# The Impact of Leader's Block

The impact of leader's block is not restricted to the leader. The leader doesn't operate in isolation; therefore, leader's block has a ripple effect on other leaders, the team, peers, family, friends and ultimately, the organization.

Many books and articles focus on the impact that leaders have on their teams and organizations, be it good or bad. Yet there is not enough information on how the external environment, circumstances and scenarios impact the leaders themselves. For example, we all know about the impact of a disengaged manager on the team, but we don't know how or why they begin to feel disengaged. As this book is for leaders, from the leaders, I have done my best to gain insights into the minds and hearts of leaders as they go through leader's block.

The impact of leader's block on leaders is far more profound than we know. These are successful people who are used to being on top of their game. To the world, these leaders are the epitome of success with fancy designations and fulfilling personal lives. To spectators, they are high up on the corporate ladder. However, those suffering from leader's block don't feel like this as they know that they are not performing to their fullest potential. During this phase they start to experience lower confidence and self-doubt. This inner noise translates into the leaders becoming irritable, short tempered, moody and volatile, which impacts them and the people around them. It affects their performance, decision-making and ability to focus, and before long, the leader begins to doubt his or her abilities. When leaders lose confidence, or are not performing at their best, they are prone to making hasty choices and impulsive decisions.

Going back to my experience, I recall walking out of my manager's office feeling like a loser. I had lost confidence in my ability to lead a team, which was my biggest strength. I felt that I had not only let myself down but also my team, my manager and the organization. My instinctive reaction was to resign, as I thought I was not good enough to do my job any more. This phase created a big dent in my self-esteem and confidence for the next couple of months. I was cognizant of my lack of confidence when I was dealing with my seniors. I was always defending my moods, I was not transparent and I was leading in a manner that was different from what resonated within me, and I hated it. I internalized the frustration and it impacted me on a personal level. During this period, I was emotionally charged and the most innocuous things or situations, such as bad traffic, could act as a trigger. I found myself swearing and becoming distraught at the smallest of things.

When experiencing leader's block, leaders find themselves to be more vulnerable. Since leaders are unsure of themselves, they can end up changing jobs, which may not be the best solution. They are blocked and dissatisfied with their current situation and therefore respond positively to soliciting calls from recruiters and executive search firms. Some of them give in to the temptation of moving to another job only to regret it later as it doesn't solve the issue; it is only a band-aid solution.

Karen, senior manager of a boutique risk consulting firm shared, 'It was the time when I was really frustrated in my job and wanted to get out of it somehow, and when my prospective employer came with a fancy designation and lucrative offer I couldn't resist. Looking back, that was a temporary fix, as that decision was not made with the right mindset or frame of mind. And I do regret it!'

Leader's block impacts the temperament of leaders. Some find themselves feeling sad as it takes away the joy of going to work. Some feel their stress levels increase and some find it hard to relax. Fundamentally, they are all losing interest in things that they feel passionate about. For example, Neville, the chief HR officer of a media company, acknowledged that people around him became concerned when he refused to go and watch a cricket match. This was no ordinary match. It was the final between India and Australia in a one-day tournament. Most people who knew Neville could tell something was wrong.

In this phase, the performance of leaders is impacted. They are not the best version of themselves—their leadership style, their commitment levels become suboptimal. If their natural style is empowering and encouraging, then during this phase they become execution-focused and distanced. They are out to prove how right they are and how wrong everyone else is. Leaders tend to become self-obsessed and defensive. That can have a negative bearing not only on the people around them, but also on the business.

The strategy head of a big insurance company shared that after he and his team realized that their strategy would not give them the results they were hoping for, they recognized that they could either continue with the same plan or make some big changes in their approach. Even though he knew the right thing would be to make the changes, he took the easier path of continuing with the same strategy. He began to reinterpret data, along with managing and aligning people to get their support. In his heart he knew he was wrong, but it was tough to accept that he had made the wrong decision. He didn't want to look like a failure.

Similar to my experience, many leaders experience a lack of confidence. It shows up in different ways for different people. For some it slows down their decision-making ability as they find themselves questioning their judgement far too often, to the point of being indecisive and impacting the business. Some leaders make ill-informed decisions and stick by them. As I shared earlier, some leaders withdraw from conversations and participation.

The impact of leader's block spills into the personal lives of leaders as well. The moods are carried home and impact their families. What Frank, the executive vice president of a midsize energy company in Europe, shared moved me and made me realize that we often ignore this side of the story. 'I think my combative nature was probably new to me. I was not only defensive but also combative at work. It was one of the few times in my career when I took home very negative feelings. What you take home are the things you talk about, and if what you are talking about is all negative, you build up a significant amount of animosity towards the individual and environment. Its effect on me was broader than work, because I put everything I had into my work. And when your work is not where it needs to be, it's very impactful to not just your day job but to the rest of your life. You can make a correlation that when you have writer's block or leader's block, it does affect your whole being. If you're truly a leader, you are invested in what you are doing, and if you are not able to perform fully and there are attributes that are blocked, it's a very tumultuous time. So, yes, I brought it home and my mood and tenor about everything I did carried over to my family, my life. It does have a significant effect—that is the personal side of this story.'

I could see that this incident had had a lasting impact on him and that he was struggling to keep his emotions in check, even as he was discussing it with me.

During the course of my research, it was amazing to hear leaders reflect on this time in their career and be objective about it. Some of them accepted that their behaviour during this phase could have hurt their reputations. As Elly, director of operations of a technology platform company, mentioned, it made her cringe to think about her behaviour during that phase. She said she was not equipped to handle the rejection when she was not promoted as per her expectations. Her immature reaction had actually confirmed to her manager that he had made the right decision and that she was not ready for the big role.

I would summarize that leaders going through leader's block experience an overall creative slowdown—their efficacy, efficiency and effectiveness are all negatively impacted.

## Impact on the Team

It's no secret that managers have an enormous impact on the teams they lead, either directly or indirectly. There is enough empirical evidence to prove that.

Hay Group[1] is a well-respected company in the field of HR and leadership, and this is what their

---

[1] According to research on leadership style and climate at Korn Ferry Institute, https://www.kornferry.com/solutions/products/talent/talent-assessments/leadership-styles-and-climate.

research says: 'Business performance can improve by up to 30 per cent when employees experience a great climate: energizing work, a positive atmosphere, feeling part of their team's success. And a leader's behaviour is the biggest factor in creating the right climate for their team.' So there is a direct relation between the leader and team performance.

The first impact of a blocked leader is on the team's morale. An uninspired leader cannot inspire the team. A demotivated manager cannot motivate the team. A lost leader cannot direct the team. The scepticism, disengagement and low energy of the leader can leave a lasting imprint on a team, leading people to switch teams and departments, or leave the organization.

Going back to my personal experience, my team was impacted as I was not spending enough time with them. I was disengaged and distanced, which made them feel lost and without direction. They thought that I wasn't interested in them and their career progression. It not only troubled them, but it also adversely impacted their performance. A few of them even contemplated moving to another team. Remember, this was the team that had stood up for me and questioned my manager when I was passed over for a promotion. Imagine the impact my block had on them to push them to move from one end of the spectrum to the other.

The negativity of leaders spreads faster than wildfire, and the team is always watching them. As leaders we cannot afford to have a 'bad day', let alone bad weeks or months! A leader's mood swings are picked up by the team, and it impacts the environment, which becomes non-conducive for creativity, collaboration or innovation. Seasoned leaders do a good job of managing their emotions and are careful not to expose them very often, but as humans we all have our threshold. Even though the teams may not see the changed behaviour, they can sense it. Zoe said that her teams could sense her frustration. Her teams and her peers could see that she was not engaged and she was sure that this impacted them adversely.

Nancy, a senior leader at a fast-moving consumer goods (FMCG) company, confided that her team was definitely impacted as decisions weren't being made fast enough. She stated, 'It was not my usual style and the team expected me to behave as per my reputation of a fast executor. I was more circumspect during this time and there was a little uncertainty for everyone.'

During this phase, most leaders become transactional, tactical and micromanagers. Therefore by extension, the team also becomes task-oriented and short-term-focused, which takes away the creativity and spontaneity from their work.

As leaders we know that when we empower and inspire others, and give them the opportunity to contribute fully, people bring their full selves to work and thrive in that environment. When we give limits, constraints and criteria, and become dictatorial about how we want to execute our business, we lose the ability to create a high-performance team. When we are blocked we start operating from that space of control.

The product head of a big technology major, whose leader's block was triggered due to her supervisor, said, 'I feel that some of the structures or approaches that I took and some of the messages that I delivered were not allowing those around me to succeed, and it really stifled creativity; it became all about executing a plan and not about achieving excellence in the business. It created a culture where we were managing expectations versus excelling, not being transparent about our business and not being inclusive about how we managed our business.' As she reflected, she felt that her team had seen the changes in her behaviour, though she didn't realize the intensity of the changes and its impact at that time.

Leaders from smaller organizations feel that the impact of leader's block on their teams and organizations is greater than it is in big establishments.

Teams in smaller set-ups are more perceptive to their leader's moods and attitudes due to their proximity. They also have a high dependency on leaders for their success and careers. The teams start to get nervous when they see or sense their leader behaving differently; they start to get worried about themselves and their careers.

Interestingly, some leaders said that they expressed their moods and attitude more openly with their peers and their managers than with their teams. For many, their team members were like their children. As model parents, they did not show their bad moods to the children. But their behaviour was definitely more obvious to their peers and managers. They stopped participating and contributing. They were more disengaged in meetings and conversations. They were not shy of showing their moods and their blocked participation.

I remember reading about a leadership model based on leaders and the environment. It talked about the environment that teams experience versus the environment leaders experience. The best leaders were those who created an environment better than the one they were experiencing. But it is human nature that if one is not experiencing a good environment, it is likely to be passed on in many ways.

I received a great insight while speaking to Paddy, the head of HR at a financial services company. He was going through a phase of leader's block and, interestingly, he experienced the impact of this phase through another (probably) blocked leader! This example reiterates the fact that leader's block has a negative impact on the people around the leader as well.

Paddy shared, 'I tended to be a little more irritable, a little more cynical. It was a struggle for me when I had leader's block; perhaps it was also due to the company I kept. I was noticing that every conversation with a particular individual was very negative and that this individual was actually not helping me. His constant complaining, cynicism and negativity accelerated my decision to leave the organization. Now I can reflect on it and say it was instigated by the company that I was keeping. It was a leader who wasn't inspired, who wasn't as engaged and trustworthy as a leader should be, and this was transferring to other leaders as well. It was damaging the whole organization.'

His story confirms my belief in what Jim Rohn famously said: 'You are the average of the five people you spend your time with.' And since we spend most of our time at work, the people whom we work with play a big role in our overall being.

There are two appropriate quotes that sum up the impact of leaders on their teams:

'The speed of the boss is the speed of the team.'
—Lee Iacocca
'A leader must inspire or his team will expire.'
—Orrin Woodward

## Impact on the Organization

An organization is the sum total of all its leaders and teams. If its leaders are blocked and not performing at their best then imagine the impact this will have on all aspects of the business. Remember, leader's block is like the flu, it is contagious and can spread very fast. The impact ranges from poor decision-making to loss of business to disengaged and unhappy teams to negative environments.

Let's start with the most significant component or differentiator of the organization: its culture. The culture of an organization is broadly shaped by how its leaders behave and display what they are trying to achieve. For example, if an organization wants a culture of innovation, but it penalizes its employees for taking risks, then innovation cannot flourish. It is also true that the culture of an organization is driven from the top down. It may sound like a cliché, but leaders are expected to 'walk the talk'. When leaders are blocked, the culture can be impacted rapidly, especially in smaller organizations. The culture of creativity, driving innovation, spontaneity and taking risks are all adversely affected.

Gallup, the world's authority on employee engagement, refers to this phenomenon as the 'cascade effect'. The *Gallup Business Journal*[2] noted that employees who are supervised by highly engaged managers were 59 per cent more likely to be engaged than those supervised by actively disengaged managers. The cascade effect states that employee engagement is directly impacted by their managers' engagement, and that the managers' engagement level is directly impacted by their managers' engagement. The cascade effect works in both directions—when a leader is disengaged it has a domino effect and the results are severe. Imagine a leader who is heading a division of 3000 people. When their direct team is impacted by their behaviour, it trickles down to other teams very quickly, so effectively, all 3000 people are impacted directly or indirectly.

For those of us who are rational, pragmatic and result-driven, I have identified two tangible and

---

[2] Amy Adkins, 'What Separates Great Managers From the Rest', Gallup report (2015).

distinct metrics that can help measure the impact of leader's block on the organization. These are the most-tracked and talked about metrics by all organizations and consulting firms, and they don't come as a surprise: productivity and attrition. For our purposes, the impact on productivity can be measured in terms of the cost of the unproductive time of the leader experiencing leader's block and the impact on attrition can be measured in terms of the cost of hiring someone to fill the position vacated by a leader who quits as a result of leader's block. In reality, however, the implication and impact of leader's block is much wider as this doesn't include the cost of the impacted teams. We will explore that later in the chapter.

When employees are not performing at an optimum level, it has a huge impact on the productivity of the organization. The impact is amplified when this happens to leaders. Leadership positions come with large salaries and benefits, so when you translate that loss of productivity into dollars, the cost is alarming.

I have based this calculation on the widely accepted research done by Gallup. According to Gallup's State of Global Workplace[3] report, on an average, 18 per cent

---

[3] 'State of the Global Workplace, Gallup report (2017–18).

of an organization's workforce is actively disengaged. Gallup describes an actively disengaged worker as someone who is unhappy and unproductive at work, and liable to spread negativity to co-workers. In other words, they are people who don't like their jobs and aren't afraid to let others know.

Now this is slightly different from leaders experiencing leader's block as being disengaged is only one element of the overall impact and leader's don't make their disengagement known to others. But given the pervasiveness of leader's block among leaders, it is worth looking at its cost and impact.

Gallup[4] found that actively disengaged employees cost their organization an additional 34 per cent of their salary. Let us apply this to leader's block. The block typically lasts between three to nine months (and up to twelve months in some cases). Let's take the median as four months, which means these leaders are unproductive for four months. If the median salary of these leaders is $100,000, it costs the company $34,000 per leader for that year. In a large organization, even if 10 per cent of its leaders experience leader's block in a year—and that 10 per cent can equate to fifty leaders conservatively—

---

[4]  Steve Crabtree, 'Worldwide, 13% of Employees Are Engaged at Work', Gallup report (2013).

it can cost the company a whopping $1.6 million in a single year.

It's simple maths. Below is a table identifying this impact, and we can do the calculations according to the company size and the number of leaders.

## Calculating the loss to an organization due to leader's block

| Company | Number of leaders | 10 per cent experiencing leader's block | Annual salary (median) | Duration of leader's block (unproductive months) | Loss of productivity (per person) | Total loss of productivity in a year |
|---|---|---|---|---|---|---|
| ABC | 500 | 50 | $100,000 | 4 | $100,000/12 x 4 = $33,333 | $33,333 x 50 = $1,666,666 |

Remember, these figures are conservative. Further, I am convinced that more than 10 per cent of a company's leaders experience leader's block, given that every leader I have spoken to has said 'yes' to going through it at least once. Also keep in mind that the number of leaders in mid to senior management will be more than 500, and in turn the salary of these leaders would be higher than $100,000.

That is a huge cost for organizations to ignore!

The above metrics take into account only the leaders who are experiencing leader's block. As we know, the teams under these leaders are also impacted and therefore we can multiply these metrics by 'x', with 'x' being the number of impacted team members. Let us assume each leader impacts ten people; the numbers one gets can be mind-boggling, as shown in the table below.

## Calculating the loss to an organization due to the impact of leader's block on the teams

| Company | Number of leaders | 10 per cent experiencing leader's block | Annual salary (median) | Unproductive months | Loss of productivity (per person) | Total loss of productivity in a year | Total impact (each leader impacts 10 people 50*10=500) |
|---------|---------|---------|---------|---------|---------|---------|---------|
| ABC | 500 | 50 | $100,000 | 4 | $100,000/12 x 4 = $33,333 | $33,333 x 50 = $1,666,666 | $33,333 x 500 = $16,666,500 |

No organization today can afford, or would like to lose, $16 million over an issue that is under its control. I will share more about the role of organizations with regard to leader's block in a later chapter.

Let us now look at the other tangible impact: the cost of attrition. If the organization doesn't support leaders experiencing leader's block, then one of the actions they take is to leave the organization.

According to a recent survey by the Society for Human Resource Management (SHRM)[5] on

---

[5] Research report by the Society for Human Resource Management (2014). SHRM is the world's largest human resources membership organization with 2,75,000 members in 160 countries.

employee retention, losing a salaried employee who makes $60,000 per year will cost the company between $30,000 and $45,000. The core revenue loss is attributed to recruitment and training of a position replacement. The study drilled deep into the expenditures and headaches associated with employee turnover, such as advertising for an open position, interviewing, training and low productivity from new employees who are learning the ropes.

Imagine the magnitude of this number in the case of a leader at the mid or senior level who is drawing double or triple that amount. Let us put this in perspective: a leader who makes $120,000 per year will cost the company between $60,000 and $75,000 in losses. So if two or three leaders leave an organization due to leader's block, that cost increases to over $100,000. If you add that number to other intangibles such as thought leadership, client relationships and morale of the team, it becomes a sizeable loss. As I mentioned earlier, blocked leaders can also induce attrition, so it is not only their cost of attrition but also the cost of replacing team members who leave.

While these metrics display the tangible cost of leader's block to the organization, the impact is deeper than the mere financial cost. It is difficult to measure the effect of leader's block on the overall health and environment of the organization in tangible terms. Nonetheless, the impact is significant enough not to be ignored.

All this may sound very daunting, but the idea is not to create a grim picture. Instead it is to highlight the importance of recognizing and acknowledging leader's block. There is a silver lining to every dark cloud. There is good news about leaders' block— like the flu, it is temporary and it is treatable. As an executive coach, it is my job to look for solutions to obstacles and there are multiple ways to overcome leader's block. In the next few chapters we will talk not only about ways to overcome leader's block but also about the preventives to reduce the frequency and intensity. Remember, leader's block helps build immunity, as you come out of it stronger and wiser!

Leader's block is contagious. It impacts not only the leaders but also has a bearing on those around them.

# 3

# The Internal Triggers

In the next two chapters I will explore the possible triggers for leader's block. We will discuss what circumstances, conditions, environment and kind of people can cause leaders to lose that focus, passion and drive that are an integral part of them. There could be multiple factors at play instead of just one reason.

Based on my interviews and conversations with hundreds of leaders, I have broadly categorized the triggers into two types:

a.  Internally Induced: These are related to factors that are more internal to the leaders, such as role fatigue, the leader's personality or expectations of themselves, the willingness to unlearn and learn or personal reasons.

b. Externally Driven: These are related to external circumstances, such as the quality of a supervisor, transitioning into a new and bigger role, the environment, or macroeconomic factors that are out of anyone's control.

Even though I have labelled them differently, in reality, most, if not all, triggers are interlinked. For example, a leader may get blocked due to external factors, which could get aggravated by his personality of being in control. Similarly, the transition into a new role may be complicated by the type or quality of the leader's supervisor.

Let us first explore the internal triggers.

## Role Fatigue

Familiarity breeds boredom.

Akki, the senior vice president of a telecommunications equipment company, has been with the same company for the last twenty years, and during those years, he has held four distinct roles. This is how he described his typical cycle: for the first year in a new role he would be excited and anxious about whether he would be able to pull it off or not; in the second year he would start getting into the groove and enjoy the role; by the end of the third year he would start to get bored with what he was doing; and in the fourth year he would start to look for something different, something exciting. While he had been lucky to get new roles before his boredom got to him, in his last role he wasn't so lucky.

In this specific case, his manager and he were butting up against each other. They had very similar skill sets and liked doing the same type of work. Akki didn't have the freedom to expand his role and go beyond his job description as his manager wanted to protect his own role. Akki stayed in the role for three years and in the end he had a conversation with his manager that he said he won't forget. He said, 'I told him that I wanted to look for a new role and my manager said that I could take on some of his responsibilities. I asked him two straightforward questions: "Who goes to Alan's (the president of our division) staff meeting? Do I go with you or do you go alone?" He said he goes alone. My next question was, "Who goes to the CFO's staff meeting?" He said he would. I said, "You know in that case you're doing the job, I'm not, so I will look for a new role." And I walked out. I always remember that because I think those two questions clarified everything, not just for me, but for him as well. I started to plan my next role

from there on and the next nine months weren't fun.
I had totally shut down inside.'

There are multiple reasons for role fatigue, a
common one being the boredom that sets in by virtue
of doing the same job for X number of years. I say X as
that number can be different for different people—for
some boredom can set in after four years, for others
after six while some continue to enjoy their job even
after ten years. My view is that it's not so much about
being in a role for X number of years, it's about the
creativity and challenges offered by the role. If there
are no new products, no creativity, no challenges
and performing the role becomes about maintaining
status quo or seeing only incremental changes, then
boredom can set in quickly. Role fatigue could set in
when there is no mental or intellectual stimulation
in the job, where the role is repetitive with very little
scope for learning or improvization. It's also linked
to the environment or the culture in an organization
or a department or even a team, which doesn't allow
the leaders to explore or express their creativity and
hence leads to boredom more swiftly than usual.

For me, role fatigue set in after five years in the
job as that role wasn't helping me grow. All my key
performance metrics were green, but I was beginning
to feel the slowdown. I was slipping into autopilot
mode, and we know that being on autopilot doesn't

create anything new. I was finding my job repetitive and boring. I knew my business and processes well, I was performing my role fairly automatically, not thinking hard about every single move, and I guess that's why I was efficient. This boredom at work eventually led to my becoming disengaged and distanced from my team.

While role fatigue is mainly driven by the nature of the challenges in the role or the number of years in a role, I also found that it can be driven by personality types—some personalities feel the role fatigue faster than others as they are constantly seeking an adrenaline rush, new challenges and exploration. I will discuss more about such personalities later in the chapter.

I spoke to Wendy, head of Asia-Pacific business development for applications at a major technology company. She was beginning to feel the 'lack of excitement', and based on what she shared, I sensed that she was facing the onset of leader's block. Wendy had been in her role for three and a half years. She had grown the business by almost 50 per cent year-on-year, and she was very proud of this achievement. There had been a steep learning curve and excitement, and she felt that she was living up to her potential. At the time we spoke, her stretch target was 60 per cent growth in the business, and she said that she had a good idea as to how she and her team would meet that number. She was pretty confident in fact.

However, she also said that she was beginning to feel that she was repeating past achievements and that the steep curve she had experienced in the beginning was starting to plateau. What she said next surprised me. 'If I don't do anything about it, I see myself potentially running into a leader's block. I see a lot of inertia. I'm repeating myself, repeating the behaviour that has been established. The thinking process has become programmed because I have learnt the skill and I don't challenge myself much. It's becoming a very smooth ride; I do need to pay attention, but I feel that I'm comfortable taking my mind off it. This could be dangerous in some ways because I'm not challenging myself,' she asserted.

I was intrigued and wanted to know more. I asked her how she was feeling about where she found herself.

'Honestly, I think externally nothing is visible, my team doesn't see anything, they see me as engaged and focused, but that's because this is a practised skill. The dilemma is inside, it's all internal to me, and I wonder how much I am challenging myself intellectually and how much I want to learn something new. I feel like there's a strong yearning in me to learn new things,' she said.

I asked Wendy if she had any ideas about how she could avoid a potential leader's block. Were there any actions she could proactively take to prevent a leader's block?

She responded, 'First, I want to make sure that my current business is in good hands. Once I do that, I want to take some time off, I'm thinking maybe three months. I am still debating whether to take time off completely or do a rotation in a team I want to learn something from. I think it will change context and definitely energize the part of my brain that I am not using. So, these are the two things I'm thinking of, but to do this I need the support of my manager and my organization.'

I was struck by Wendy's earnestness. Even though she was feeling stuck, she still cared deeply about her job and responsibilities. That's a sign of a great leader.

Speaking with her made me think that there could be many leaders out there who might find themselves at this crossroads. As they go through this dilemma, who do they speak to? Who do they discuss it with? If they do discuss it with their managers, what is the outcome? Are organizations really open and ready to have this kind of conversation with their people? How do they proactively deal with it?

What happened to Wendy? Did she manage to escape the leader's block? Did she have that conversation with her manager? Did she take those three months off? I was curious to find out, so I went back to her after a few months. I will tell you more about her in the next chapter.

I have noticed that in general after a few years, roles tend to become stale. Leaders are successful, they implement great ideas, build strong teams, but they find themselves intellectually stalled. Everything seems like a chore instead of a new learning experience. Also, as one rises in seniority, there are fewer roles to grow into within the organization, and from a leader's perspective mobility could be restricted due to professional and personal reasons. Organizations have a big challenge to solve—how to constantly create and provide new and exciting avenues for leaders.

## Self-induced or Self-inflicted Triggers

For me, this is the most fascinating reason for a leader's block. As an executive coach, I see this in many leaders I work with. I call this the problem of smart and ambitious people who set very high benchmarks for themselves and their careers, which if they fall even slightly short of, they take as a personal failure. This self-induced problem can be due to multiple reasons. It could be due to personality types or setting very high standards and expectations, or resistance to making changes in themselves.

At times, some of our key strengths can become self-sabotaging in strange ways. When we look for perfection and set very high or unrealistic targets or goals for ourselves, even a small failure can make us unhappy, dissatisfied and blocked. This constant perfectionism can instil a fear of failure, and therefore, we may not try something new or change our behaviour, which can be a deterrent to our progress. Another indirect impact is that if the people around these leaders are not able to keep pace with their constantly rising benchmarks, it can become very exasperating for both the leaders and their teams.

One such personality I spoke to was Sean. He described himself as someone who was overall dissatisfied. He said he felt that way because he was always questioning why he was not doing something different. As a result, he was pushing himself constantly, and when he didn't get the movement he expected in whatever he was doing, whether at work or personal goals, he became dissatisfied.

He told me that his personality had been such from a very young age. He would always define success as, 'Am I ahead of my peers? I mean my contemporaries or the people with me in grade school, high school and college, and by many counts

I consider myself an absolute failure while I have done well in certain measures.'

Let me give you some more background on Sean. He has been a successful investment banker for twenty years, leading a big portfolio across the globe. Anybody who is familiar with investment banking will know that it is a fast-paced environment with a lot of excitement as every quarter, every month and every day is different because you are working with new customers and projects.

He told me that he began to feel dissatisfied when he started to do his job almost effortlessly; there was no challenge left in it. There was no monetary challenge because at a certain level the compensation doesn't grow exponentially. He wasn't driven by the intellectual challenge, he wasn't driven by the challenge of finding new customers. So putting all those factors together, his job had started to become a slow grind. 'I knew it was all internal, it was self-inflicted and it lasted a year before I decided to do something about it,' he said. Sean had finally quit his job six months before I interviewed him, and he had started his own company. His personality hadn't changed, but he had found an avenue to continuously 'move the ball forward'.

The spectrum of personality traits is well described by one of the tests done by Hogan Assessments.

Hogan Assessments is a popular leadership consulting firm that evaluates your personality at the workplace. It measures your personality traits, risk of career derailment, core values and cognitive style. It conducts a test called Hogan Dark Side (HDS), which talks about how your strengths can become your weaknesses when they are stretched to one end of the spectrum. For example, passion is an excellent trait, but when it goes to the other end of the continuum it can become rage.

According to HDS, when the pressure is on, the line between strength and weakness isn't always clear. Drive becomes ruthless ambition; attention to detail becomes micromanaging; perfectionism become an obsessive disorder. Similarly, being excitable may help you display passion and enthusiasm to co-workers and subordinates, but it can also make you volatile and unpredictable, which is taxing for others. The dark side of one's personality can derail careers.

Under this model there are eleven traits that have the potential to work against us if they are not monitored and checked. These eleven traits are being bold, cautious, colourful, diligent, excitable, dutiful, reserved, leisurely, mischievous, sceptical and imaginative. Having the awareness is a great way to keep ourselves in check, especially if we are more prone to any of these traits compared to others.

Another person who was constantly looking for excitement and change was Sandy. He was a seasoned leader who had moved from a banking job to a corporate job and then finally to a start-up in search of greener pastures (as he described it). This is how he explained his journey: 'I consider myself a driven individual, I have always done things that have excited me throughout my academic days and my career. The challenge that I have faced is that I get bored very easily. When I start something new I am enthusiastic to learn and then when there is nothing new to learn I get bored, which is true for most jobs. The issue is that I get into this phase faster than the average person, where I feel the mental fatigue; I have no energy and the fire in my belly drops. I consider this my weakness, and I have to constantly guard against it. In fact, all of the changes I've made in my career are driven by this constant search for something bigger and better. I have now realized that it's probably my personality trait. So I have to guard against frequent changes as every change is preceded by this phase where I am totally blocked and shut down and that's no fun.'

Sean and Sandy are classic examples of personalities where strength and the desire to constantly look for excitement could become a weakness and lead to dissatisfaction. Listening to them also made me think that perhaps after a certain stage in our lives, designation, money and social status cease to be priorities or things to chase. Our focus shifts to the quality of the roles we perform. It becomes more about contributing, making a difference and an impact. I am not saying that titles are not important or don't matter, but they are not substitutes for a fulfilling piece of work. To the external world these leaders are meeting their key performance metrics and producing the desired results, so the dissatisfaction is not obvious. Internally, these leaders constantly feel dissatisfied or that they can do more.

It's ironic that while on the one hand titles and designations aren't that important for leaders, on the other, recognition within the company is important. If leaders are overlooked for a promotion or recognition or a big assignment, it breeds self-doubt, so external validation is critical. They become self-effacing because they hold themselves to such high standards that they take it as a personal failure. So again the suffering is self-inflicted.

I hear a lot of similar stories from the leaders I coach. Leaders say that when they are getting the business results and managing their teams well, they feel they are ready to move to the next level; but if that doesn't happen, it leaves them feeling bitter. Amar, a senior director of risk management at a technology company, is one such leader that I coached. When he wasn't promoted as he expected, he waited for six months, and when he was passed over for promotion again, his first reaction was that the situation was unfair. He was ready to engage in a debate to prove that he deserved a promotion. He became very negative and complained to everyone he spoke to. He took it as a personal failure and found himself blocked for the next four or five months; that was when he engaged me as his coach.

As leaders we sometimes look at ourselves in the binaries, in black or white—either we are rock stars or complete failures. We forget we are humans who can hit temporary dry patches. Sometimes a lot of success in the past sets the expectation that whatever made us successful will continue to make us more successful, so we keep doing the same thing. But at times that is not enough because at higher levels of leadership, the dynamics change. What brought you success earlier will not bring the same level of success moving forward. When we don't achieve success at the rate we are used to, we start feeling frustrated and look at the world as either being against us or unfair. We are not able to understand objectively why we didn't get that job or that promotion, we are not prepared to handle the rejection and we act in ways that don't benefit us.

As we become more senior, we resist making changes in ourselves, whether to our operating style, thinking style or leading style. In today's constantly changing environment there is a need for agility, adaptability and flexibility, and this can become overwhelming for the leaders who are used to operating in certain ways. Leaders can continue to apply the same style of managing instead of learning new tricks. For example, if some tasks are not getting done, then they can increase the frequency of monitoring instead of changing the conversation completely. In a strange way, a history of strong success can stop us from unlearning and relearning. Because we have been successful, asking for help appears as a sign of weakness, so we try to manoeuvre into new territory with our old skills.

In fact, as leaders we could use these instances of challenges and changes as learning moments in our growth and development journey.

My close friend Victor is a senior partner with one of the top three audit firms globally. He shared with me that in audit firms, talented auditors sometimes struggle when they are promoted as partners. I asked him why. He told me that going from being a member of the audit team, managing two or three direct reports, to running a business was a big change. The shift to being the key person responsible for bringing in the business, as well as making sure that the team was well led, could be daunting for many as they were not always prepared to change their old ways of working. Leaders struggle trying to juggle different balls, manage the team, day-to-day affairs of the business and get business as well. He said it can be unnerving to have the spotlight on you; he himself had struggled for the first five or six months after his promotion before he started getting comfortable. He shared a very interesting example of that shift: 'I would generally ask my team for ideas in meetings as a way of collaborating and getting consensus; later I got the feedback that they were expecting me to give them directions! I realized that this was a different ball game and I had to play it differently.'

This scenario is quite common in technology companies where most of the leaders are technically very strong, but struggle when they have to start leading big teams, run a business vertical or get new business as that requires a big shift in their approach and mindset. Since leaders come with the baggage of past success, there is a lot of pressure on them to learn the ropes fast. Leaders could either get aggressive or defensive as the pressure starts to get to them and this is where they find themselves getting blocked.

It is the self-created persona and image that stops them from being open to learning and saying, 'I don't know' or 'I need help'.

## Personal Reasons

As you become more senior in an organization, two things start to happen: firstly, the roles open to you in the organization start to become limited as the pyramid narrows, and secondly, your mobility can become restricted due to personal reasons such as health issues, your spouse's job, children's education or the need to take care of aging parents. I know many leaders who don't want to move from their base city or country as their children are in critical years of school, and therefore they are ready to stay on in a job even if they are not very happy; they are okay not making any changes as they don't want to uproot their families.

I interviewed Jack who had moved to Singapore as his wife had got a great opportunity to lead the Asia-Pacific region for her company. He realized that his job as an analyst in a consulting firm was not a perfect fit for him, and he definitely wasn't performing at his best, but he continued in it as the assignment was an important one for his wife. He is a 'trailing spouse', which is a term commonly used to describe people who relocate because of their spouse's job. In situations like these, there are sometimes limited choices for the trailing spouses and so, even if they are not happy in their jobs, they stay on as they are doing it more for personal reasons.

My husband, who was heading business development for a major shipping port in the US, took a desk job for two years when our daughter was born. Even though his heart was in sales, he made the change as he wanted to spend more time with both our children. He doesn't say he was unhappy, as it was a personal choice, but he did not enjoy the work and felt the slowdown. He knew it was temporary and that he was doing it for a special reason.

There are many leaders who don't want to uproot their families and move to a new location and, therefore, will remain in their current jobs even though they are not satisfied. Given this constraint, how can they make changes in their current scenario? How can they unblock themselves? What is the best way out? We will find answers to these questions in chapter six.

When we find ourselves blocked, our tendency is to blame the external environment, things and people. But as we reflect, we discover that a lot of our blocks are internally induced. We have control over them. The key is to be aware and acknowledge them.

In the next chapter, I will talk more about the external factors that can trigger a block.

> Even though every leader and their circumstances are unique, there are a few common themes that trigger leader's block.

# 4

# External Triggers

In the previous chapter we talked about the internal triggers for leader's block. These are reasons that to a large extent are within our control. They could be due to our choices, personalities or due to our circumstances.

In this chapter we shall explore the external triggers for leader's block. These are reasons that are driven by factors outside our direct control.

## Quality of the Supervisor/Manager

We have all heard that people work for people, not companies. People leave managers, not companies. We also know that supervisors play a big role in the life of an employee. Relationships with supervisors define the way people feel and perform in their jobs. We know that the success of any employee in any organization is usually correlated to the supervisor and it is not any different for someone in a leadership role. There are enough studies and research to illustrate that one of the top reasons for attrition, low employee engagement and performance is the quality of the immediate manager, and senior leaders are no exception to this rule.

Being led by a leader who doesn't provide enough resources or guidance, or a manager who micromanages and does not trust the team, can be challenging and stressful. Many supervisors don't do enough to recognize and appreciate their teams, which makes it difficult for the team to enjoy its job. What do we do when our manager doesn't see the big picture or doesn't want to rock the boat and wishes to maintain the status quo? It's never easy when we don't know what our manager is expecting of us; it is like going for an exam every day.

We have all been impacted by good and not-so-good managers in our careers. Interestingly, both types help us learn something. Early in my corporate journey, I had a manager who was bright and intelligent but had poor interpersonal skills. He was volatile, would scream in meetings and no one wanted to come into his line of fire. I worked with him for two years and learnt what not to do when it was my time to lead a team. That was my best learning!

As I sat across from Frank, the executive vice president, he said that he had experienced several phases in his thirty-year career during which he had felt he was blocked or certain attributes of his leadership were blocked. I asked him if there was an instance that stood out for him, one that had had the maximum effect on him.

He said, 'The phase that had the most impact on me was the relationship with my supervisor, which was not inspiring me. It was one that didn't allow me to be empowered to do my job and took away a lot of my energy and enthusiasm. While I was leading a large organization, clearly, I was not inspired to the degree that I needed to be. I still worked very hard, but the intangible qualities were probably missing from that job for a period of time.'

I was curious to know what it was about his supervisor that had made him feel that there was a difference of opinion. Had there been a clash of values?

'The big disconnect was that I didn't feel I was trusted or valued for my contribution. I felt that instead of positive reinforcement, there was more of a fear factor that was instilled in the relationship around performance. Those things, over time, drew energy away from me, and my inspiration and my commitment to my job at the time was probably less than optimal. I would say personal attributes like inspiring others and being creative were definitely blocked. I was in a different mode of leadership at the time, that's the only experience in my career where I wasn't contributing fully,' he explained.

At that time Frank was an executive vice president and reported to a very seasoned leader. I mention this for two reasons. Firstly, even if we hold a senior position, it is still imperative to have a good working relationship with a manager in order for us to perform to the best of our abilities. Secondly, sometimes even the most experienced leaders, such as Frank's manager, can have a blind spot.

The clash or differences with a manager could be over operating styles, thinking styles or leading styles. As long as these differences help the team and business due to the diverse points of view they bring, they are healthy. But when these differences become an impediment to a person's performance and progress, it's time to take note. Sometimes a manager's appetite for change and new ideas could be different from ours, which might kill our excitement to drive change, implement new ideas and explore new opportunities.

However, a clash of values with a manager can be a complicated situation as it not only impacts us professionally, but personally too. What do you do when you don't believe in what your manager values, what the manager is asking for or how the manager is leading? It's one thing to not always agree with a strategy or business decision, but if how the leader handles disagreements and conflicts, or treats other people clashes with your values, then it's a tough situation.

I spoke to Elaine, an associate at a consulting firm who had faced such a situation, and was keen to know what happened and how she dealt with it.

'I had this constant internal battle that I am compromising my values. I was being rewarded for doing well, but I was not completely bought in, I was not a 100 per cent committed because I was not feeling good. This was a case regarding selecting people for promotions and new roles; my manager worked more on personal choices rather than meritocracy. I felt that from a leader's perspective I was jeopardizing my own values and morals to some extent. I had been on the brink of "can I last any longer and still make this work and not jeopardize my own values" or should I just quit? I got lucky—fortunately, he was fired!' she said.

It is not just the managers themselves who impact us. The environment that managers create within the teams and around them also affect us. I have noticed that sometimes managers can get insecure if they have a team of strong people. They don't know how to handle such a situation and often will create unhealthy competition amongst the team members, which doesn't help anyone. I am sure quite a few of us have experienced that!

Everyone that I have spoken to has mentioned that their managers have had a huge impact on their overall performance and being. The issues people have faced varied from working for a micromanager, to working for someone who didn't promote meritocracy to dealing with a manager who didn't appreciate and acknowledge the team to working for someone who always took all the credit. The list goes on. The fact is that almost all of us have been impacted by the managers we have worked for and, depending on the individual, this impact could have been positive or negative.

I believe there are two things that people teach you—what you should do and what you should not do. From my perspective, when leaders work with managers who are not great, there is a huge learning opportunity. We learn to be better managers as we know the pain of being managed by an insecure, incompetent or a non-trusting supervisor.

Another insight I had as I reflected on all the stories that leaders had shared about their managers was that perhaps those managers were going through a leader's block. After all, they were in those positions because they were smart people, but maybe something was stopping them from being great managers. It points to the pervasive nature of leader's block and the fact that no one is immune to it.

## Transitioning into New Roles

Leaders are often tested when they transition into roles that are bigger or more complex than the ones they have done before, or those that are in a domain different from their expertise. Transitioning is not always simple and straightforward. There are multiple articles that say that 20 to 40 per cent of leaders fail during transitions.

Based on my interactions with leaders, I discovered there are two factors that impact the self-confidence of leaders as they transition. First is the enormity and scope of the new role and the second is the environment of the organization, department or the team that the leader is transitioning into.

David had been successfully leading the business development for his company until he was asked to head a new division. It was a new domain not only for him but also for the organization. It required a new way of thinking and operating. He said that he struggled with the transition and had to start learning a new domain from scratch as there was no existing process or framework. This made him feel powerless. In a candid conversation, he said, 'I froze! This was totally out of my zone and I was stuck with my old style. It took me three months to realize that I needed help. Then, finally, I reached out to some of my peers in the industry to learn more. I wasted all that time and went through an unnecessary ordeal for those months before I gathered the courage to ask for help.'

It is not uncommon for senior leaders to find it difficult to unlearn and relearn things. Big egos and insecurities are at play. Leaders don't want to look and sound short on any competency or skill, even though it is not humanly possible to be an expert in everything. Asking for help is looked upon as a sign of weakness by leaders, and it takes a lot of courage to admit that they don't know something, especially if they are masters in their domains. That is why many of them struggle as they transition into something new.

Interestingly, another challenge faced by leaders when taking on a new big role is the famous imposter syndrome. This was made popular by the second-most-watched Ted Talk in 2016, given by Amy Cuddy. In her book *Presence*,[1] she states, '. . . the general feeling that we don't belong—that we've fooled people into thinking we're more competent and talented than we actually are—is not so unusual. It's not simple stage fright or performance anxiety; rather, it's the deep and sometimes paralyzing belief that we have been given something we didn't earn and don't deserve and that at some point we'll be exposed.'

As leaders take on positions of increased responsibility, they are likely to experience the imposter syndrome. It is the feeling that we have fallen into something that we are not sure we can handle or have the necessary skills to fulfil. The organization will tell you that they have faith in you, but it is our own fear of failure that impacts confidence levels and, therefore, our performance. After speaking to many leaders, I realized that contrary to the general belief, imposter syndrome is equally prevalent in both male and female leaders. Perhaps they don't project it that much. Well, that's a conversation for another day or another book!

---

[1] Amy Cuddy, *Presence* (Orion, 2016).

Malti, a senior operations leader at a major oil and gas corporation, shared her transition story. She went from managing the logistics for the company's gas marketing business in the US to taking over the supervision of the gas marketing business globally. She called this a leapfrog change in terms of responsibility, ownership, scope and personal management. Malti said, 'My new role had a lot of personnel challenges where we performance-managed people. It's never easy to fire someone. Even if you have done it before it's hard. But if you haven't done it before, it feels almost impossible. I had to make business decisions which had a direct and significant impact on the business and the people. That got me very nervous. I was leading a division of 300 people and the feeling of being watched closely was quite overwhelming! I started to doubt myself and felt totally blocked. I realized that I had to overcome the self-doubt before I could instil that confidence in the organization.'

It's true that as leaders we have to believe in ourselves and have the conviction to successfully execute our vision before anyone else believes in it. With the right coaching and mentoring, this transition can become smoother and easier for leaders.

Another critical aspect of transitioning is the environment of the new organization. After the first few years of our careers, we realize that we work for reasons more than just our salary and perks. We look to align our work to a bigger purpose. We are susceptible to leader's block if our purpose is not aligned with that of the organization. What if we believe strongly in innovation, taking risks and creating something new, but our organization is risk averse, bureaucratic and believes in maintaining the status quo? It is not always about values, it could also be the pace of change, style of operating, the products, and maybe even the people. As we become more experienced and seasoned, this alignment becomes more important because in the initial stages of our career we are still figuring out our own purpose and bigger goals.

I shared in the first chapter how Zoe was struggling with the pace of change in her new organization. She thought that it was out of her control as it was driven from the top. She was exasperated by her team's reaction and attitude towards the adoption of new technology and new ways of working. That misalignment caused her frustration and became an impediment to realizing her vision for the department and the organization.

Another story that struck a chord with me was Nancy's, a senior leader at an FMCG company. Her experience captures many facets of the challenges leaders face during transitioning to a new role—the manager, the team, the environment of the division, the transition road map and much more.

When Nancy stepped into her new role, everyone had high expectations of her since she had already built a solid reputation for herself within the organization. In her new role, she came up against new dynamics that she hadn't experienced before. Firstly, her two new bosses couldn't stand each other. They had an openly antagonistic relationship. Although she personally got along fine with both of them, she felt like the child stuck between two warring parents. The second dimension was her team. Since she was leading an important business, she had a team of star performers for every function, whether it was finance, HR, product supply or research and development. Ironically, while the team members were all stars, they did not add up to a star 'team'. There were too many egos at play.

She shared a few examples of her ordeal and how it impacted her. 'One time there was an overlap of dates for two important conferences in different locations. Instead of agreeing on which conference I should attend, my two bosses literally cut me in half. So out of the three days of conferences, I did one and a half days in Singapore and then flew to Geneva and attended one and a half days there. This is the extent to which they couldn't agree between themselves; in fact they couldn't agree on anything,' she said.

It became very clear to Nancy that she had a tough job on hand. There were ego clashes below her and ego clashes above her.

When she began her one-on-ones with her team, she realized that everybody had the 'I'm perfect' attitude and that it was others who needed to change. According to Nancy, the actual business challenge was not difficult; her real battle was the organizational challenge and that required her to engage very differently. She revealed, 'My internal talk was am I being too neutral, am I not taking a stance? It was like my confidence was shaken. I also knew that I didn't have the cover from either of my bosses, so I was constantly convincing both of them about what I wanted.'

She struggled for six months and described it as the loneliest period of her career. I think that's another example of a classic leader's block. I couldn't help smiling when she said, 'Now the good news is that since it was so painful, I figured out very quickly that I was having a block and started the work to overcome it.'

Nancy's story is one case out of many that I heard in my interviews with leaders. It made me wonder how and why organizations underestimate what it takes to ensure a smooth transition of leaders into new roles and positions. Can organizations be more supportive of leaders who are making these transitions? Can organizations be more deliberate about it?

## External Factors

In this section, I have put together reasons that are beyond our control, and yet they have an impact on us as leaders. If not handled well, they can result in a leader's block. These are a combination of various factors such as macroeconomic factors, business decisions or even personal reasons. As humans, we know that life is uncertain and that we can't control everything. Similarly, as leaders there are a few things that are beyond our control. For example, our organization may be acquired or macroeconomic factors may make us redundant or our personal circumstances may restrict us in the choices we can make. All these situations can be a temporary impediment to our progress and can cause us to become frustrated and feel stuck. It was insightful for me to speak to few leaders who had faced some of these situations.

What happens when the business landscape changes due to big events such as the collapse of capital markets or the slowdown of the global economy? In the last ten years we have seen a lot of change and disruption across the globe within the business environment, including the global recession, which impacted many leaders across the world.

The International Monetary Fund (IMF) defines a global recession as 'a decline in annual per-capita real world GDP, backed by a decline or worsening of one or more of the seven other global macroeconomic indicators: industrial production, trade, capital flows, oil consumption, unemployment rate, per-capita investment, and per-capita consumption'.

The 2008 global recession was by far the worst of the four post-war recessions, both in terms of the number of countries affected and the decline in real world GDP per capita.

Many leaders I spoke to had witnessed the aftermath of the recession and the slowdown. Many of them found themselves blocked and stuck during this time. There was little they could do to salvage the situation; some changed tack while others waited for the time to pass.

My conversation with Garry, founder of a risk and compliance organization, was telling of such an environment. He told me that his company had been on a growth trajectory when Lehman Brothers collapsed and they were forced to take a pause.

They had raised money from the market, which put them under tremendous pressure to perform, and they had to pivot quickly, make big changes in the costs, lay-off people, keep the right people and keep them motivated. There was an internal tussle among multiple stakeholders—investors, the board of directors, the chairman—and some investors wanted to take out their money as they found the business too risky. This caused a decision pause. All these issues arose due to multiple factors that were out of everyone's control. Garry said, 'I was not able to balance and manoeuvre this complex environment. I felt as if all my faculties had slowed down. I was in that phase for almost three months before I got back on track.'

Another effect of these macroeconomic factors or slowdown was retrenchment. No one saw it coming, a few leaders lost their jobs and some left in anticipation. The fear of retrenchment made some leaders make choices that were not optimal for them. Some leaders hung on to their jobs even though they were not fulfilling. It had a bigger impact on leaders who didn't have the skills to make a job shift quickly, and there were quite a few in this category.

One of the leaders I spoke to had been part of a successful banking institution and had to leave his job because his company was shutting down. He said most of the organizations in financial services had been his clients and it was very awkward for him to approach them for a job. He described this as a tough period for himself, not financially but mentally. The hurt of being at the receiving end and taking it as a personal failure was immense. This was the story of quite a few leaders from the capital markets during that period and they were not alone—there were hundreds, if not thousands, of leaders impacted by the 2008 financial crisis.

Today, with all the technological disruption and the competition from start-ups, organizations are compelled to restructure in order to stay agile, effective and relevant. Mergers and acquisitions are a big part of that strategy, as stated in a *Harvard Business Review*[2] article published in January 2018, '. . . in the last eleven years, there have been over 500,000 M&A deals—more than in any such period in recent history.' Apart from the changes in business models, financial statements and organizational structures, the biggest effect of these restructurings has been on the people. The impact of any kind of restructuring is felt by leaders. Some lose their existing portfolios, some are aligned to another manager and some even

---

[2] Benjamin Gomes-Casseres, *Harvard Business Review* (December 2017 and updated in January 2018).

become redundant. This is a period of uncertainty and ambiguity for leaders and without enough support and guidance they begin to feel lost. If that period extends for more than four to six weeks, leaders find themselves in a block.

When I spoke to Satya, the programme leader for a financial services company, he said that when his company was merged there was a striking shift, it felt as if he had become a guest in his own house overnight. He had been heading a big transformation project at the time and, in his first review meeting with the new management, he was asked to redefine the business case for his project. 'It left me totally outraged, it seemed like all my hard work and effort was being wiped off in a jiffy,' he said. It was just the first of such interactions for him. A few weeks later, his project was put on hold. Satya shared that in the months that followed, he had no job to speak of. He would go to the office and do random work. This phase was agonizing for him, and that was his leader's block.

Contrary to the general view, the impact of such business decisions is also felt by the decision makers themselves. Neil was the co-founder of a company that was acquired by a publicly traded organization, and he was one of the people to sign off on the deal. His situation was quite unique as he went from running the company to being one of the employees of a big organization. He soon found that the buck no longer stopped with him, and this was the biggest change for him. Previously, every decision he made had a bearing on the company. It could make or break the company. Now, at best, he would get a call from the CEO agreeing or disagreeing with his judgment. He stopped getting the adrenaline rush that he would experience earlier and that was a significant demotivator for him. He shared that the first six months after the acquisition were excruciating for him, and as many leaders have said before, the pain was aggravated by the fact that he had to put up a brave façade for his team.

Based on the reasons and triggers for leader's block, I would say that there are four types of block:

a. Systemic: This is driven by the environment in an organization, which includes the types of roles, the quality of supervisors/managers, transitioning into a new role and the culture of the organization.
b. Personality: This is mainly self-induced, common among smart and ambitious people who are constantly searching not only for bigger and better things but also for constant excitement and perfectionism.

c. Situational: This is caused by unique external factors such as the macroeconomic environment, a global slowdown or business decisions such as mergers and acquisitions, restructuring or a sell-out.

d. Personal: This is driven by personal choices due to health, family or any other personal circumstances.

As we have seen, multiple reasons can trigger a leader's block. It is the new normal and there is no getting away from it permanently. However, the key is to recognize it, acknowledge it and then work to overcome it.

In the coming chapters, we will talk about the impact of leader's lock and how to overcome it.

On a separate note, after listening to founders of start-ups such as Neil, Garry, Sean and many other entrepreneurs during my interviews, I realized that there was another dimension to the phenomenon—leader's block for entrepreneurs is quite different from leader's block for their counterparts in the corporate world. The triggers for an entrepreneur's block are mainly internal, the duration tends to be shorter and more intense, and even the consequences and impact are more drastic. For an entrepreneur, experiencing a leader's block can be compared to a baby getting the flu—it requires immediate attention and a lot of care. To go into more depth on this is probably the subject of another book!

We cannot control everything. The key is to select the right interventions to overcome external or internal triggers.

# 5

# The Symptoms of Leader's Block

For Andrew, the global procurement leader of a medical devices company, mornings would start quite early. He lived in the suburbs of New York, and it would take him more than an hour to get to work. His drive to work was always busy, as that was when he would talk to his team in the Asia-Pacific—it was early evening for them. He told me that talking to his Asia-Pacific team was always energizing for him as most of the action around technology, business and innovation was in that part of the world. The calls were not necessarily work related. They were a means for him to spend time with the team as he would do with his team in New York. He loved to chat with them, find out what was happening with them and create a sense of belonging. He typically made three to four calls during his drive to work. However, during the two months before I spoke to him, he had found that slowly the number of calls had gone down to two and then one and even that stopped after a few weeks. It wasn't that he didn't like talking to his team any more, but he just didn't feel like talking. He was trying to avoid thinking about work.

His drives to the office became long and boring. Even his favourite music failed to cheer him up. By the time he reached the office, he felt exhausted and depleted of energy.

That was how Andrew felt during the time he was experiencing leader's block. It didn't stop with his commute to work, his disengagement stayed with him in the office as well. He found himself shutting down and withdrawing into a shell; he stopped participating in meetings and putting his hand up for new projects.

Andrew is not alone. Leader's block manifests in external behaviour and each leader reacts to this phase differently. But when one studies these behaviours closely, one sees a pattern emerging. Leaders who have a high level of self-awareness can identify these patterns and symptoms not only in themselves but also in others. They realize that these behaviours could be a sign of trouble if not checked.

The narrative of the leaders during this phase is negative, they tend to become more cynical, the words and phrases they typically use are 'it has always been done like this', 'I know how this will work', 'it won't work', 'I have done it before'. There is scepticism and the chats at the water cooler are no longer fun or gossip sessions—they are off-putting. The blocked leaders unconsciously make the environment around them negative.

Malti, whose experience I shared in an earlier chapter, said she became so negative that it not only surprised her team but her husband as well. She was always trying to prove that she knew everything and was defensive about her actions. 'Thank god those interactions were not recorded,' she said.

As I have mentioned before, leaders are creative people and the leaders I spoke with proved me right. They were all very descriptive and imaginative in the way they described the symptoms of leader's block.

Chris, the extrovert leader who loved to talk about everything under the sun, felt as if he was in a box and someone had put him on mute. He felt restricted and stifled. He felt boxed.

For Frank, the executive vice president, it was the boredom that was getting to him. He told me that as unprofessional as it sounded, it was true—he found himself mindlessly browsing the Internet. Whether in meetings or during conversations, he was bored and his way to fight that boredom was to surf the Internet. It came as a big jolt to him when one day he found himself looking at Facebook at 9 a.m.! He knew something was wrong. This continues to be the biggest telltale sign for Frank. He has realized that if he finds himself surfing the Internet more than usual, then something is not right.

Akki had a similar story to tell. 'I couldn't believe I was doing this—I was snoozing my alarm a couple of times every morning and would refuse to get up till my wife would literally pull the covers off. My wife started to get worried; she thought I was not well. It felt like the days when I didn't want to go to school. You wouldn't think you would hear this from a senior vice president of a multibillion-dollar company.'

It might sound counter-intuitive, but during this phase, leaders tend to work harder than usual. It seems that they are out to prove their relevance and worth; it is also their way of keeping themselves busy. It is a different matter that working harder doesn't get them the desired results as they focus on the wrong things. They end up micromanaging, becoming transactional and paying attention to things that are not important. Their calendars are filled with review meetings—half of those meetings don't require the leader to be there! One leader jokingly shared that once he even sat in on a vendor meeting for the demonstration of a coffee machine for their office. The focus shifts from being strategic to being transactional; they miss the woods for the trees. They don't take out enough time to reflect and step back, and they avoid acknowledging what is really going on.

The corporate world teaches us to fake it very well. Even though we may be feeling bored, disengaged, lost and cynical, we have to put on a brave front with our teams and stakeholders. This internal turmoil can be painful. Motivating the team while feeling demotivated, showing direction while feeling lost, inspiring the team while being uninspired can be challenging and exhausting.

Imagine you enter the lift in your office building feeling drained, shoulders slumped and lost in thought, and a staff member enters with you, looking all bright and excited. They greet you: 'Good morning, Jane! How are you?' You are forced to smile, look enthusiastic and say, 'I am great. How are you?' You start the day with a lie and this trend could continue through the day, so by the end of the day you are drained from telling all those lies!

Depending on their personalities, circumstances and environments, leaders react differently to leader's block. Some leaders shut themselves out, even from their friends, as they don't feel like socializing and want to internalize what is going on. Others go out with friends to keep themselves distracted and busy—it is an escape for them.

The key is to recognize these behaviours not only in ourselves but also in our team members. If this pattern of behaviour continues for an extended period of time, for more than four to six weeks at a stretch, leaders will know that something is wrong.

Leaders who have learnt how to draw lessons from their leader's block recognize these patterns of behaviour and symptoms, so if it comes around again, they are able to catch it early and work on it before it becomes a full-blown block.

The symptoms are clear in the way leaders sound, feel, act and look during this phase. They exhibit behaviour that is not part of their personality and therefore it feels and looks strange to them and others. Sometimes they don't see this pattern of behaviour clearly in themselves, but others can spot it. It could be their team members, managers, friends and family, people who know them well. The symptoms don't show up only at work, they spill over into the home too. Leaders become irritable and quick-tempered; their families see and feel the shift.

'This was an extremely painful period for me,' said the vice president of a fast-paced technology company. 'I was constantly torn between listening to my heart and head. I felt so guilty about not doing my job full-heartedly, the company was paying me big money after all, and I was just whiling away my time and going through the motions. I was sitting on decisions and being the bottleneck. I almost hated myself, but it seemed like I had no control over myself—my heart was not in the job.'

Nancy, senior leader at a FMCG company, shared, 'I felt as if one of my bosses was waiting for me to fail, so I had to constantly prove otherwise. I became quieter and more cautious as I didn't want to be proven wrong, I was not being myself. It was affecting me personally, my confidence was shaken. I was afraid to try new initiatives or take risks as I didn't want to fail.'

Satya, the programme leader whose company was acquired, shared that his confidence took a beating, he was unsure when dealing with his seniors and he internalized the frustration. It was a vicious cycle as he lost confidence, which made him lose focus, which in turn impacted the quality of his output, which then reflected badly on him.

The senior manager of a boutique consulting firm, Karen would sit for hours staring out of her window. Initially, she couldn't understand why she felt so zapped and lethargic all the time. She was drinking more than six to seven cups of coffee a day to shake off the lethargy. She found her behaviour to be quite volatile and erratic. For example, she would be vocal and talk a lot for two days, and then for the next three days she would just clam up.

Elly, the director of operations at a technology company, shared that she became very defensive about her work and organization. She was always defending her moods, withholding information, not being transparent and leading in a way that was not her usual style. A few leaders said that during this phase, they did more managing than leading. The phase was like a rollercoaster ride for many.

I received some fascinating responses when I asked the leaders if they had a visual description of how they felt during this phase. The leaders were quite ingenious and the descriptions ranged from being insightful and deep to being humorous in some cases. This is what they said:

a. I felt like a tree in autumn—no leaves, no life, but the tree is there, and the leaves will be back in spring.

b. It was like being lost in a desert, looking for an oasis.

c. Calm, still water, absolutely still, no ripples.

d. I felt like I was entering a dark, unfamiliar and huge room. I didn't know what to make of it.

e. It felt like being placed in a box, trapped, trying to draw attention.

f. I was like a snail going into its shell.

g. I felt like I was inside a tunnel and could see only a small light at the end.

h. It felt like being locked in a huge cage and trying to bend the iron bars to come out.

i.  It was like being lost in a maze, constantly hitting a dead end and not finding the way out.

The common thread in these descriptions is that they are all reflective of the internal quandary that the leaders experienced. It takes a high degree of self-awareness for leaders to recognize and acknowledge the internal dilemmas they face while experiencing a leader's block. This internal turmoil, if not attended to, can have serious repercussions on the leaders—it could lead to a burnout. These kinds of internal dilemmas and turmoil are difficult to detect early on. In the initial stages, these symptoms could be attributed to the regular Monday morning blues. It's only when these Monday blues extend to a week, and then to a couple of weeks more or longer, that the leader is forced to think that something could be wrong.

During this phase, leaders can feel quite helpless. They feel alone and often think that if they share what they are going through with anyone it could be seen as a weakness. The fear of failing, or appearing to fail, is frightening. That is perhaps how the corporate world teaches its leaders to act. But, as humans, we have a threshold of internalizing our emotions and, after a time, these emotions need to find a vent.

For people who are more expressive, these symptoms are displayed more through external behaviours. A common external manifestation is the way people walk. Many of the leaders I spoke to felt they had lost the spring in their step and that their shoulders drooped or slumped. They almost found themselves dragging their feet. Even wearing branded, high-end suits and shoes didn't help!

Shauvik was an investment banker and an avid movie fan. He was passionate about making movies and acting in them. He would fund his filmmaker friends to make short films and he would act in some of them. He said that when he acted he forgot the world around him and that it was the closest to attaining nirvana. During the time he was experiencing leader's block, he stopped his association with films. His filmmaker friends would call him to watch movies or invite him to act, but he wouldn't go. This was scary, he said. His friends thought something was seriously wrong with him. He didn't feel like going out and doing what he loved the most and it got him worried.

Zoe from the first chapter described her state in a rather poetic way, 'Sailing in turbulent waters, you see the lighthouse way down. The waves go up and down, but I also see calm peaceful water. It feels a little lonely, though I know there are other people.'

Once we have experienced leader's block, it is easy to see it in others. It makes us more perceptive as leaders and we are able to pick up the signals in our teams, and in those around us. It is critical and beneficial for organizations to create awareness about these symptoms so that they can be detected early and attended to accordingly.

In his famous bestseller *What Got You Here Won't Get You There*,[1] Marshall Goldsmith wrote about habits and behaviours that hold leaders back from reaching the top. In the book, he mentions twenty-one habits.

---

[1] Marshall Goldsmith, *What Got You Here Won't Get You There* (Hyperion, USA, 2007).

Out of these I have selected six habits and behaviours that were mentioned by leaders who had experienced leader's block.

a.  Winning too much: The need to win at all costs and in all situations.
b.  Making destructive comments: The needless sarcasm and cutting remarks that we think make us sound sharp and witty.
c.  Negativity or 'let me explain why that won't work': The need to share or negative thoughts even when we aren't asked.
d.  Withholding information: The refusal to share information in order to maintain an advantage over others.
e.  Making excuses: The need to reposition our annoying behaviour as a permanent fixture so people excuse us for it.
f.  Clinging to the past: The need to deflect blame from ourselves and on to events and people from our past; a subset of blaming everyone else.

You will notice that all these habits and behaviours are tangible and externally focused. They are about being defensive and can be easily seen and experienced. The leaders I spoke to all talked about these habits in one form or the other. These behaviours, when exhibited by leaders, are great telltale signs that something is wrong.

The key is to recognize these behaviours.

A few leaders felt like victims—they felt that everyone was out to get them. They had the sense of being taken for granted and taken advantage of. It's fascinating that the symptoms ranged from being aggressive and out to get others to feeling victimized.

One thing was common: for leaders, these behaviours were not normal and they often felt that they didn't recognize the person they had become. Clearly, for leaders it is not an enjoyable period—they don't like the person they see in the mirror every morning and yet they live with the situation for anything from three months to a year. Imagine how painful that period must be—to see a worse (worst) version of yourself. And since these behaviours are atypical, they are exhausting and draining for the leaders.

Leaders with high self-awareness can recognize these digressive behaviours, but their ability is impaired when they are in this phase as they try to justify themselves. The more tangible and practical way is to have a mechanism to get candid, genuine and brutal feedback. As we have all experienced, sometimes as leaders we know that something is wrong, but we are not able to put our finger on it. It would be much easier if someone could tell us about the shift in our behaviour.

This feedback could come from people who watch us and interact with us from close quarters, be it a family member or peers at work. After all, this behaviour is more visible to others and equally impacts them.

Amar, the senior director of risk management, shared that the changes in his behaviour were picked up quickly by close friends and family. 'My wife was the first one to notice that I was talking about the problems rather than the solutions (which was my natural style) most of the time. She pointed that out to me and I blamed it on the stress of a critical project at work. After a few days, a similar comment was made by one of my close buddies. That is when I realized that my behaviour was not completely internalized and it was showing up in ways I was not even aware of. I realized that I had to act on it before it started to impact my team and the organization.'

I have mentioned Elizabeth Wiseman's book *Multipliers* in an earlier chapter. In addition to defining multipliers and diminishers, she breaks the definition of diminishers down into five disciplines.

I like to call these five disciplines the five traits of diminishers. They are:

a. Hoarding resources and underutilizing talent.
b. Creating a tense environment that suppresses people's thinking and capability.
c. Giving directives that showcase how much they know.
d. Making centralized, abrupt decisions that confuse the organization.
e. Driving results through personal involvement.

These five traits are very similar to the behaviours that those experiencing leader's block display.

She also says that most people fall along this spectrum, so you could shift from being a multiplier to a diminisher and vice versa. When a leader is experiencing leader's block they can become diminishers during that time. So when leaders start to behave like diminishers, they know that they are either heading towards or experiencing leader's block. It's a great way to catch ourselves and others.

Sandy, the leader of a start-up, told me that he would lock the door to his office, put his feet up on the desk and sit for hours like that. He just didn't feel like talking. This was coming from a leader who was vivacious and known for his witty one-liners. He said he felt alienated and sad. He didn't like this version of himself but couldn't understand why he was feeling the way he was. He said that now whenever he has the urge to lock himself up in his room, he gets into a self-reflective mode as he knows something may be brewing. It's a signal for him.

While Sandy found himself shutting down, Akash, the vice president of a pharmaceutical company, would do anything to keep himself distracted and not think about the issue at all. He said he started going out more frequently with friends and family. Even on weekdays after work he would call his friends and go out. This was an unusual trait which surprised his friends. Akash was a busy man and for him to be doing this so frequently was not normal.

David, meanwhile, said he felt like he was swimming upstream all the time. He was putting in a lot of effort without much result. He chuckled as he told me that he didn't know how to swim.

There are two types of symptoms that manifest when a leader is experiencing leader's block: internal and external. There are plenty of books and articles that talk about the external behaviours of leaders, whether it's Marshall Goldsmith's *What Got You Here, Won't Get You There*, or Elizabeth Wiseman's *Multipliers*, or the article 'Off the Track: Why and How Successful Executives Get Derailed' by Morgan McCall and Centre of Creative Leadership.

Not many people have talked about the internal struggles that a leader goes through in this phase. I have tried to dig deeper into the internal symptoms of the leaders. What is it that they feel as they go through this phase? In most cases leaders struggle more with the internal turmoil as it's harder to share, explain and to overcome. Once leaders have a good understanding of these symptoms, they can recognize these patterns of behaviour in themselves and also detect them in the leaders around them.

During the time that I was experiencing leader's block, I remember I became very defensive, task-oriented and also disengaged and distanced. I didn't feel like talking and interacting much with people at work or socially. Now, if I find myself getting defensive about my actions or distancing myself from colleagues, friends and family members too often, I stop and reflect—it's usually a sign of the flu and I know it needs my attention.

To summarize, these are the key symptoms that can help us recognize leader's block:

a.  We go into autopilot mode.
b.  We start to sound negative, cynical and sceptical.
c.  We work harder and not necessarily smarter.
d.  We start to micromanage and become transactional.
e.  We become irritable and short tempered.
f.  We start to feel lost and directionless.

If you continue to experience or display these symptoms for a few weeks, it's time for some medication as you may be heading towards the flu!

> The symptoms are early warning signs for leaders to recognize and acknowledge that they could be headed towards leader's block.

# 6

# Overcoming Leader's Block

Remember, leadership is a journey. Every journey, whether it is via road, air or water, will have its own speed breakers, turbulence or high tides. The leadership journey is no different. The key is to work through the obstacles and challenges and continue the journey.

In the previous chapters I shared the reasons that could trigger leader's block and its impact on leaders, teams and the organizations. I also explored the root causes of leader's block. In this chapter, I discuss the solutions. What can we do to overcome leader's block? In life there is no one perfect answer; similarly, there is no one definitive way to overcome the block. Different leaders may use different methods, strategies or tactics depending on their situation, personalities and environment. The actions could range from making a small shift in behaviour to more intense changes like quitting your job. It is up to each leader to choose what works best for them, and they may need to do multiple things to get over leader's block.

In due course everyone finds their way. Some may take longer than others, but ultimately, they get over leader's block. The issue is that if we continue to ignore the symptoms and don't take any action, the consequences can be severe—we could burn out, end up in an unpleasant place or continue to be miserable for a long time. Therefore, it is imperative for us to take action to overcome this malady.

The suggestions to work through the block are based on what I have learnt from coaching leaders and my interviews with leaders across various industries around the world. Throughout the book, I have given snapshots of our conversations and the anecdotes shared to explain various aspects of leader's block. Based on my findings, I have put these actions into five broad categories, with an easy acronym to remember them by—BLOCK. These actions may seem simple and obvious, but as we know it's not the knowing, it's the doing and being that's arduous!

Let us now work to unBLOCK the leader's block.

## B: Big Picture

When leaders are going through leader's block, they tend to feel lost as if they are in a maze. They often feel confused and experience a lack of clarity and objectivity. They may need to step back and look at the big picture regarding their goals and objectives. They should ask themselves, what is it that I want and how is my current situation stopping me from getting there? Am I doing anything that is hampering that big goal? What do I need to do to get closer to my goal? It is difficult to do this on our own as it's tough, if not impossible, to be completely objective and honest with ourselves. We need someone to probe us, nudge us, provoke us and challenge us to think deeper and come up with answers. That person could be a mentor, a coach or a trusted adviser.

My dear friend, mentor and a renowned professional speaker, Fredrik Haren, helps people, especially speakers, find their 'inner theme' through one-on-one sessions. In these sessions, Fredrik works with people to find their passion, their key strengths and helps them understand how these are aligned to what they do. These sessions help people gain clarity on their life's purpose and identify the areas to focus on so they can get closer to it.

For example, Fredrik's inner theme is 'humanity to the power of ideas' and his mission in life is to help maximize the potential of humanity through creativity and the sharing of ideas. Helping others find clarity around their own inner themes so that they too can go out into the world and spread their message helps Fredrik be true to his own inner theme.

When I coach leaders, we spend a substantial amount of time on finding and defining their North Star or 'compass of life'. This is especially important for senior leaders, as by this stage most of their worldly (materialistic) career aspirations such as financial goals, social goals and status goals have been met, and they are in search of deeper meaning.

Simon Sinek's TED talk, which is the third most-viewed TED talk ever, encouraged people to be more conscious of finding their WHY. He said in his talk, 'Everyone has a WHY. Your WHY is the purpose, cause or belief that inspires you. Knowing your WHY gives you a filter to make choices, at work and at home, that will help you find greater fulfilment in all that you do. Why you do what you do?'

Having a clearly defined purpose or why is good for everyone. It's a great strategy for people who are constantly looking for bigger and better things—defining their purpose will help them stay focused and grounded. It also gets us to look at our lives more holistically. Our work is one part of our life, but what about our satisfaction, happiness and contribution? Once we have defined our purpose, it becomes easier to put things in perspective and take action accordingly. When we have clarity on where we want to go, then it is quite straightforward to set the GPS and find the correct route. We can also make changes to our route as we go, especially if one path is closed or is bumpy.

One of the leaders shared that when his to-do list becomes long and overwhelming, he steps back and recalls the big picture. Then he steps back in and is able to sort that list in terms of prioritization and importance. Leaders sometimes get so caught up in running day-to-day operations that they can miss the big picture. They tend to become more transactional, especially when they are going through a leader's block. It is phases such as these that almost force them to make a pit stop and ask some basic questions: Where am I going? What do I need to do?

The next time you find yourself getting lost in the weeds, ask yourself these two questions:

a. What is my purpose? My 'why'?
b. How is this particular situation helping me get close to that goal?

If you haven't yet defined your 'why' then it's time to work with a coach or mentor to help develop one.

## L: Let It Pass

It may sound counter-intuitive, but sometimes the best thing to do is to wait for the tide to pass. It is the best solution when things are beyond control, and getting through such a phase is simply a matter of time and perseverance. Having this mindset helps in getting through blocks that are caused by things beyond our control such as macroeconomic situations, disruption, mergers and acquisitions. As leaders we are biased towards action. Our first reaction is to act, but taking actions that are not thought through can hurt our career.

One of the first things people do when they are not happy with their supervisors is to think of quitting. But that may not be the perfect solution; they should not give up on their job so easily. What would they do if they got a difficult boss again? Similarly, if you are in a role that is not very fulfilling, but you know you have to stay in it for personal reasons, you could either choose to be miserable about it, complain about it or let time pass patiently.

If you recall, Frank was struggling with his supervisor and it had a huge impact on him personally and professionally. I asked him how he overcame his leader's block. He said that one day it dawned on him that he wasn't going to be able to change the course of the current environment, and this freed him from dealing with it. He said that the realization made him less sensitive, and he was better able to handle the issue. He picked himself up and got back to his normal leadership style. It was the wise thing for Frank as he knew the situation was temporary and he wasn't going to be in that role forever.

As humans, and more as leaders, we are always trying to be in charge. We think we have the ability to control anything and everything that comes our way, and we believe we are capable of handling it perfectly. But that is not true; there are many things that are out of our hands. Sometimes not doing anything is harder than taking action, especially for leaders who are used to taking action. It requires patience, persistence and perseverance to believe that not doing anything now will help us build something solid later.

In her book *Grit: The Power of Passion and Perseverance*.[2] Angela Duckworth writes about two components that make us gritty: passion and perseverance. As Duckworth defines it, 'Grit is passion and sustained persistence applied toward long-term achievement, with no particular concern for rewards or recognition along the way. It combines resilience, ambition, and

---

[2] Angela Duckworth, *Grit: The Power of Passion and Perseverance* (Vermilion, 2016).

self-control in the pursuit of goals that take months, years, or even decades.'

I loved this book and it resonated with me, particularly her comparison of the focus on passion versus perseverance. In general, people are more focused on their passion but don't spend enough time building and practising the persistence, perseverance and patience to realize that passion. I think there is a lot of unlearning and learning for leaders here, as traditional leadership is all about being aggressive and taking action whereas sometimes what is required is just the opposite!

For cricket lovers, here is an interesting analogy. When a batsman is out of form, he tries to block the ball instead of hitting big shots. He spends time on the pitch till he gets back into the groove. At times we need to do exactly that till we get back into our zone.

When things are not in your control and you can't do anything to influence the situation, the best thing to do is to wait for it to autocorrect. Garry's company was impacted by the global recession. Instead of taking hasty action, such as shutting down or selling out, he waited. He let time pass and fortunately for him the tide turned, the disruption became favourable for his firm and he was back in business like never before.

A seasoned leader told me that she always asked herself three questions before taking any action. These could be good questions to ask ourselves also:

a. Does this opportunity help me grow?
b. What value can I add to this role/job?
c. Will it be fun?

The answer to all three must be 'yes' for her to act; even one 'no' is a NO!

## O: Opinions of People

As we have read, when leaders go through a block it reflects in their behaviour, and often, leaders are oblivious to these changes. It is through feedback that leaders learn how they are being perceived and the changes in their behaviour that they may be blind to. Taking into account the opinions of people around them is the most potent tool leaders have to help them make changes in their behaviour. I am not referring to the formal 360-degree assessments that many organizations use. I am talking about deeper responses that are more informal in nature, which come from people who are close to you, who see you in action. These could be the people at work such as your manager, peers and direct reports, or your close friends or family members. Seeking their opinion is a great way to find out if you are on the right track or if you are displaying behaviours that are not normal for you.

Somehow the words 'opinion' and 'feedback' conjure up mixed emotions. We think others are going to highlight our weaknesses and we become defensive, and therefore we may be afraid to ask for their opinion. I have heard leaders say that people don't always give honest inputs and maybe that's true. That is why it should be solicited and actioned in a way that makes the other person want to share more. If someone has given you their input on your behaviour a couple of times, but you don't make any changes then obviously that person will not give you feedback the next time you ask for it. Or if you defend your behaviour and justify why you behave the way you do then it will stop the other person from sharing the next time.

In my coaching practice I use a 'perceptions report', which was designed by my business partner Ashley Chiampo. At the start of a coaching engagement, I interview eight to ten of the leader's stakeholders. The purpose of these interviews is to gain insights about the leader in an informal, anecdotal way. I get an opportunity to ask questions and dig deeper. Based on what I hear, I look for patterns and then prepare the report highlighting the key strengths of the leader, the areas of focus and any deviation from normal behaviour. I then discuss this with the leader and often get comments such as 'I didn't realize that was how my behaviour was perceived', 'I didn't think these were my key strengths' or 'This is my development journey for the next three to five years'. Leaders find this report very valuable.

Some leaders shared that their aha moments came through candid feedback and conversations. One such example stood out for me. For Pran, a newly promoted chief HR officer (CHRO), his conversation with his boss, the CEO, was the most strategic dialogue he had ever had. His boss challenged his working and operating style by asking a few simple questions: 'If you work these long hours, when do you get time to reflect? If you are doing your team's work, then who creates the strategy and sets the direction for the company?' Initially, Pran was rattled, but after a few days he saw the merit in those questions. As he looks back, that powerful input has shaped him as a professional and as a leader.

Opinions of people who matter can help guide us in our journey. Through them we know if we are on the right track or if we are digressing from our normal behaviour and doing things unconsciously that might be hurting our reputation.

As I have mentioned, when leaders are experiencing leader's block, it is reflected in their behaviour, and this change is observed by people around them even if the leaders themselves are unaware of it. So a great way to identify changes in our behaviour is through the help of others. Some leaders are very perceptive and they pick up signs. They understand the tone of a conversation and body language, and know what people around them are feeling. They take that as feedback and prod deeper to know more.

At times, the most valuable feedback can come from unexpected quarters. I was leaving home one day when my then seven-year-old son, Samar, asked me where I was going. I told him I was going for a coaching session. He asked, 'Mama, what do you do in these sessions?' I said with some pride, 'I listen to the leaders, support them, encourage them and problem-solve with them.' Samar looked at me, a little puzzled, and innocently said, 'Mama, then why are you not like this at home?' I was taken aback. I asked, 'What do you mean?' He said, 'You don't listen to us, you are always shouting at us, getting angry at us; you don't spend enough time with us.' That was the most direct and precious feedback I have ever received! From that day on, I have been continuously working on Samar's inputs and ask both my children for their opinions on a regular basis.

As leaders, we need people around us who are not afraid to tell us where we are faltering and where we need to focus. As leaders we need to keep our eyes and ears open to the said, unsaid, expressed and unexpressed opinions of those around us.

Let us ask ourselves these questions:

a. How often do I solicit other's opinions—daily, monthly, quarterly?
b. If I do, how often do I act on that feedback?

## C: Change Lanes

When letting it pass is not the solution, then change becomes inevitable. It could be changing our role, our manager, our organization, our approach or attitude, or even our careers. Having the ability to drive or make these changes makes us feel in control rather than helpless or powerless.

The leaders I spoke to acted differently to make the changes to their situations. Leaders working in big organizations invested time in looking for internal opportunities, new projects or initiatives and tapped into their network to find more opportunities. A few leaders looked for prospects outside their organization. They reinvented themselves and embraced the opportunities that came their way. One leader told me that once she realized that she couldn't force changes to the environment, she decided to look at what was under her control. She reflected on what was negotiable and non-negotiable for her, and once she was clear on that, she decided to make changes. She looked for a new job.

Sean from the previous chapter decided to make the big shift. After a lot of contemplation, he finally gathered the courage to change the direction of his career, and he started his own company. He wanted to change the environment around him. Today his environment allows him to move the ball forward every day.

Not all changes have to be radical. Imagine a scenario where the leader really likes the organization for which he or she works. They like the role but are beginning to feel the role fatigue. They know that there are no suitable opportunities for them in the organization. But they do not want to leave the organization either. What do they do? They can continue to feel trapped and helpless or 'job craft' their role.

'Job crafting'[3] is a term coined by Professor Amy Wrzesniewski (Yale School of Management) and Professor Jane Dutton (University of Michigan) based on their research in 2001. Job crafting is defined as 'actions that employees take to shape, mould, and redefine their jobs'. It is what employees do to reimagine their job to make it more personally meaningful. Job crafting is initiated by the employee and not by the manager. There are three different techniques of job crafting: task crafting (changing tasks), relational crafting (changing relationship) and cognitive crafting (changing one's perceptions).

There are many articles that explain the benefits of job crafting, but to me the biggest benefit is the feeling of empowerment. This exercise makes you feel in charge and responsible for your job and career. It is a great enabler for job satisfaction and therefore drives performance and employee engagement for the organization. Job crafting can be a particularly valuable skill to develop when the economy or other factors prevent you from leaving your current job or when you get bored easily and are guarding against frequent changes. Like most things, it has to be done

---

[3] Professor Amy Wrzesniewski from Yale School of Management and Professor Jane Dutton from University of Michigan, 'Crafting a Job' (2001).

within the boundaries of the organization's overall structure.

As clichéd as it may sound, change is never easy, especially when it is about us. It could be our operating style, thinking style, learning style or personality. As leaders, we need to constantly unlearn, learn and relearn, but that is easier said than done. We are all victims of our habits and strongly held beliefs. In the bestseller *Immunity to Change*,[4] authors Robert Kegan and Lisa Lahey show how our individual beliefs, along with the collective mindset in our organizations, combine to create a natural but powerful immunity to change. I would recommend this book to all the leaders looking to make changes in their behaviour.

Some leaders have to unlearn their style of 'leading by exceptions' and become more hands-on with operations, while some leaders may decide to lead by setting a clear direction for their team rather than letting them deal with ambiguity on their own. Some leaders may decide to step back and not be stuck in the weeds. One leader said that he started to focus on what he was good at; he changed his approach of trying to be good at everything and

---

[4] Robert Kegan and Lisa Lahey, *Immunity to Change* (Harvard Business School Publishing, 2009).

decided to go deeper with his expertise and make a bigger impact.

In one way or another, making changes helps leaders get over their leader's block.

Before you make any changes, ask yourself these two questions:

a. What is holding me back from making changes in my behaviour?
b. Is this change going to help me in the long run?

## K: Kinship

Leadership is a long-term game and it is not possible to do it on your own. It is easier and more fun when you involve others. It can be very lonely at the top so it's important to have a group of people around you with whom you can be yourself. As social beings, we crave that sense of belonging and community, and it is no different at work. Having a community of trusted advisers, colleagues and friends at work makes us happy and effective. This group of people plays a big role as leaders try to overcome their leader's block.

Having friends at work helps us stay energized and a little gossip, a few water cooler chit-chat sessions and occasional extended lunches don't hurt anyone. On the contrary, they are great stress busters. It is definitely not wasting time! Many people might think that they don't go to the office to make friends, but when you spend almost ten hours every day at work it is natural to build connections. It's more than just about having fun, it is about creating a common sense of purpose and the mindset that we are in it together. My views are validated by prominent research and the leaders I spoke with.

Gallup,[5] in its popular employee engagement survey, posed the question: Do you have a best friend at work? The results showed that close work friendships boost employee satisfaction by 50 per cent and people with a best friend in office are seven times more likely to engage fully in their work. It has a bearing not only on the leaders but also on the organization.

Many leaders I spoke to said that having friends at work, within or outside their function, was therapeutic. They could speak openly to them as they had a good understanding of the environment. Some progressive organizations encourage and invest a lot in peer learning; they allocate a budget

---

[5] Gallup's Q12 Employee Engagement Survey asks the employees to answer 12 questions.

for people to travel and to spend time with their peers so that they have the opportunity to discuss what's going on in their areas of work and seek feedback from each other. Speaking with people who have similar backgrounds helps as they have the experience and the objectivity to look on the issue on hand.

Apart from our friends and peers, there are a few other people who can play an important role in our career, and therefore it's important to build an ecosystem and invest in these relationships.

A sponsor is our advocate, someone who is influential within the organization, creates visibility for us and puts up our name whenever there is a potential opportunity to progress our career. In today's matrix and decentralized organizations, it is very important to find a sponsor as your manager can push your case only so much. Some organizations have a structured sponsorship programme while others are creating one to benefit the employees and the business.

As leaders we know that mentors play a significant role in our careers. We have all either had a mentor and/or could be a mentor for someone else. Mentors help us, support us and guide us based on their own experience and expertise. They are the people who have been where we are aspiring to go. They help us problem-solve, advise us and are our go-to people when we are stuck or need to discuss a situation. Most of the leaders I spoke with had mentors who they turned to when they were going through leader's block. Interestingly, for a few leaders their ex-bosses were their mentors.

In recent times, we have seen a rise in executive coaching in the corporate world. There are studies that show that almost all of the top CEOs have coaches. Coaches are people who help us unleash our potential, they help us find solutions by challenging us, probing us and helping us reflect. They don't advise us, they don't give us the solution, they provide a sounding board and they serve as our mirrors. They make us examine our belief systems and help us discover our habits and behavioural patterns. For many leaders, coaching can be a life-changing experience, and I am one of those people. Quite a few leaders engage a coach to get clarity and overcome their block. There is a clear demarcation between the role of a mentor and coach. A mentor will advise you on what to do, provide you with answers, share their experiences, and will probably have had either similar experiences or a similar background as yours. A coach, on the other hand, doesn't do any of this; he or she will help you build self-awareness.

Another avenue that provides an opportunity to network with like-minded people to share and talk about common issues is mastermind groups. These could be groups that have formed based on industry, location or even interests. Most industry associations have these groups. I recently witnessed the power of these groups when I was invited to speak about leader's block at one such gathering. As I explained the topic, the attendees were relieved to find that all of them had experienced leader's block and that they were not alone in this. That encouraged them to open up and share their experiences, and some of them continued to stay in touch as their cases resonated and they wanted to learn from each other.

In one way or the other your kinship is your biggest asset and it is worth investing in it.

My two questions for you are:

a. Do you have the key people in your ecosystem to support you?
b. Who do you call when you get stuck?

We can unblock the leader's block with these five easy to remember actions. As I mentioned, no single trick will do the magic, we might need a combination of actions to overcome the block.

I had promised to tell you what happened to Wendy, head of Asia-Pacific business development for applications at a major technology company, who was on the brink of a leader's block when I spoke to her. She spoke to her manager who was very considerate and understood her situation. She took a three-week vacation to start with. Once she was back, she job crafted her role and redesigned it to expand her scope and impact. She also got involved in a global initiative, which gave her a great opportunity to learn and contribute. Wendy is an ideal case of someone who caught the onset of leader's block early and took appropriate action.

Personally, the two actions that helped me get over my leader's block were working with a coach and the opinions of my team. I gathered the courage to have a candid conversation with each one of them and asked for their honest inputs. I can't thank my team enough. Had it not been for them I would not have paid any heed to my changed behaviour and mindset, and could have continued being in denial. I was also fortunate that my manager was very supportive and agreed to sponsor an executive coach for me. Undergoing the coaching changed my life—literally! I realized the power and impact of coaching, and unconsciously it sowed the seed of my inner theme of making an impact. Little did I know that a few years later I would become an executive coach!

I close the chapter by saying that apart from taking action, we need a lot of patience and perseverance as we work though our leader's block as no action will yield results overnight.

There is good news about leader's block. It's temporary, it's treatable and helps to provide clarity. Remember the B.L.O.C.K.

# 7

# Prevention and Management

Leader's block is a real problem that leaders and organizations are facing today. In the previous chapter we talked about the role of organizations in helping leaders get through this phase. Managing leader's block is very personal and leader-specific as the threshold for fatigue, demotivation and dissatisfaction is unique to each leader. So while organizations play an important role, we as leaders need to take the onus and build practices that not only help us overcome leader's block but also prevent us from getting into it again.

Going back to the flu analogy, we know that it is not possible to build complete immunity against it. I would say that this is also true for leader's block as we cannot foresee and control all the events and circumstances to come. However, we want preventives to reduce the frequency, intensity and duration of leader's block.

We take the bitter pill for treating the flu, but then build immunity by following good habits such as washing our hands frequently, eating healthy and exercising. Similarly, there are specific actions that we can take to overcome leader's block (unBLOCK), but we also need to develop practices that will act as preventives.

Some of these practices are an extension of the interventions that we use to overcome leader's block. While those interventions—such as asking for opinions or talking to your mentors or making changes—are specific to the situation with the intention to solve the issue on hand, some of those actions can be used as preventives. For example, getting continuous feedback that is more proactive, or talking to your mentor on a regular basis and not only in times of crisis.

It is not necessary that a leader who has experienced leader's block once won't experience it again. In fact, most of the leaders that I interviewed had experienced it more than once. My hope is that through this book leaders are able to foster greater awareness so that they can not only recognize and acknowledge the symptoms the next time, but also develop habits and routines that act as preventives for leader's block.

To build immunity you have to follow most, if not all, of the practices. Doing one thing alone will not be enough. For example, if you collect feedback from people regularly but don't take time out to reflect on it then the purpose is defeated. Similarly, having a board of advisers will not help unless you leverage them.

Let us look at the practices, routines and rituals that can help us prevent leader's block.

## Recreation

I feel this is one area that is underrated and underestimated by leaders. Taking regular holidays and breaks, or pursuing a vocation or hobby, or playing a sport, is not something that leaders do or take seriously, though I must say that millennials are good at this. Taking regular breaks is one way to step back and recharge our batteries. But do we do enough?

Timothy Ferris in his bestseller *The 4-Hour Work Week*[1] says 'less is not laziness'. He talks about how

---

[1] Timothy Ferris, *The 4-hour Work Week* (Crown Publishing Group, 2007).

our culture and society tend to reward personal sacrifice over personal effectiveness. There are multiple statistics to show that about 40 per cent of people check their emails while they are on vacation. I personally know so many people who do that and I have been guilty of that in the past too. This statistic becomes interesting and ironic when you combine it with the Gallup survey results, which show that about 70 per cent of employees are not engaged at their jobs. We are not fully engaged at work and we are not fully engaged when we are on vacation. We need to do something different here!

One of the leaders I spoke with said that having gone through two major leader's blocks during his career, he has now put a mitigation plan in place. He said he 'religiously' takes four vacations a year. He says 'religiously' as he ensures he never misses them and he completely switches off from work—he doesn't check emails! For him it's a complete revamp and detox, which helps him avoid getting into a funk.

Taking regular breaks and stepping away for a while is one way to keep your mind fresh and focused. Remember, you are not doing anyone any favours by working too hard.

A few leaders said that playing sports helped them calm their mind and clear their thoughts. This got them thinking differently and is a great way to learn resilience and how to bounce back after a setback.

Similarly, pursuing a hobby such as painting, writing poetry, cycling or even coaching your son's baseball team or your daughter's football team is beneficial. One of the leaders shared that for her, volunteering at her son's school, whether for an event or for an outing, was the best way for her to relax and get away from the hectic pace of work. She described the hours she spent volunteering as being among the most tranquil ones she experienced. After a crazy schedule and stress at work, it was her getaway, and also spending time with kids helped her put things into perspective.

I know some of these suggestions and practices are simple but not necessarily easy. The key is to build and integrate them into our lives.

It may seem counter-intuitive that if you want to get ahead at work, you should make time for a life outside of it. But having a hobby is key to being able to handle work-life stress and thinking creatively. Facebook co-founder and CEO, Mark Zuckerberg says that having a hobby shows a prospective employer that you have passion and drive. In fact, it's a question most recruiters often ask candidates.

The benefits of having a hobby range from better performance to better health and reduced stress. A hobby makes us more productive and creative at work and helps us build a better attitude at the workplace. It won't be an exaggeration to say that having a hobby reduces the chances of getting into a leader's block. There are enough studies to show a correlation between having a hobby, either physical or creative, and better health such as lower blood pressure, reduced stress and fewer negative emotions.

## Reflection

Adjacent to recreation is reflection. When you take time off to do something that refreshes you, it gives you an opportunity to reflect. It lets you reflect on things you have done, you are currently doing and you want to do in the future. It's an opportunity to step back. As leaders we have a bias for action and sometimes we are so immersed in the weeds that we forget to look at the big picture.

In recent times a term that has gained popularity is 'mindfulness'. Mindfulness is paying attention to the mind, body and emotions so we can begin to approach the world with more openness and inquisitiveness. The mindfulness movement is about building greater self-awareness.

Timothy Ferris has interviewed some of the best talent in the world across the fields of sports, entertainment, business, start-ups, politics and academia. About 80 per cent of his interviewees have some form of daily mindfulness or meditation practice. Both these practices help create and cultivate a present-state awareness that helps you to be non-reactive. These practices help you to focus and prepare for the day ahead.

One of the leaders I spoke with shared a very interesting practice. He said that he talks to himself. Whenever he finds himself feeling negative or demotivated, he goes for long walks and talks to himself. The self-talk is a great way for him to get clarity. He described a funny incident about walking and talking to himself in the park close to his home, saying he got strange looks. One person actually asked him if everything was okay. Since then he started to put his earphones on so that it looks like he is talking to someone on the phone instead of talking to himself.

There are various ways to make time for reflection and there are different tools that help you to reflect. One of the ways is to write a journal. There are a lot of benefits to writing a journal. It helps you to reflect, build discipline, clear your mind, and it sparks creativity, to name just a few of them.

Stephen R. Covey, an American educator, businessman, keynote speaker and author of the popular book *The 7 Habits of Highly Effective People* wrote: 'Keeping a personal journal, a daily in-depth analysis and evaluation of your experiences, is a high-leverage activity that increases self-awareness and enhances all the endowments and the synergy among them.'

While many leaders recognize the need for and the benefits of recreation and reflection, their challenge is making and finding time for them. However, a few leaders have discovered how to do this. Some leaders block a few hours a week in their calendars and use that time purely for reflection. Some come to the office an hour before their teams come in and use that time to reflect, while some leaders use their commute time to reflect instead of checking emails or browsing the Internet. The key is to make a conscious effort to find time and make it sacred.

In his bestseller *Power of Habits*,[2] Charles Duhigg talks about how to break negative habits and build new ones. For me, the biggest takeaway from the book was the ways to grow one's willpower. When we have strong willpower we are able to establish good habits and these habits help keep leader's block at bay. These are the three effective ways described

---

[2] Charles Duhigg, *Power of Habits* (Penguin Random House, 2012).

by him to build willpower, and I use these when I am coaching leaders:

a. Do something that requires a lot of discipline: For most leaders, getting up early to exercise is a tough regime that requires discipline. But once they start doing it, it gives them willpower throughout the day.

b. Plan ahead for worst-case scenarios: As a coach I ask leaders to imagine the worst case scenario with regard to the outcome of a crucial meeting or a decision. This prepares them mentally to face the results if and when they are unfavourable.

c. Preserve your autonomy: We know that the best way to create accountability is to ask the person to set the actions. When we set our own tasks or make our own decisions there is greater accountability as compared to when we are told what to do by someone else.

## Unlearn to Learn

With all the changes in the business landscape and the technological disruptions, leaders have to be willing to change their operating style and their way of thinking, break the stereotype and be open to not only learning, but also to unlearning. They must give up their old ways of thinking and operating if they are no longer serving them. It's easier said than done as their way of thinking has got them where they are and, therefore, they have a bias for it. When leaders are open to learning they ask for help as soon as they feel stuck and don't try to solve the problem all by themselves.

We need to keep upgrading our knowledge and skills as things are changing so fast. For example, with a multigenerational workforce we cannot continue to lead in one way; we need to show more adaptability in our style. Many organizations today promote something called reverse mentoring. This is a phenomenon that was made popular by GE's CEO Jack Welch in the '90s. Senior leaders ask emerging and younger leaders to mentor them as the latter are much closer to the customers and employees, and are attuned to new trends and technology. This not only helps senior executives but also helps young leaders to network, learn the business and gain visibility within the organization.

Ryan Holmes, the founder and CEO of Hootsuite, shared his thoughts on reverse mentoring in an article: 'As a leader, one of the most empowering moments is when you're reminded that you don't know everything. There was the time, for example, when I was determined to launch an internal newsletter to connect with my employees. But during a coffee session, a new training consultant on our team pointed out that, in all likelihood, no one would read it. Instead, a short weekly video from me, posted on our internal company Facebook, would be a far better way to go. She was absolutely right, of course, and I've been making weekly CEO update videos ever since.'

There is power in being open to unlearning and learning. Constant learning helps leaders keep their jobs exciting and expand their knowledge base.

The learning mindset helps us build resilience and stops us from quitting when things don't go our way. In the *New York Times* and *Wall Street Journal* bestseller *The Dip*,[3] Seth Godin describes the dip as a temporary setback that can be overcome. His key message is to know when to quit and when to stick. He says that quitting in the short term is a bad idea since we have already invested time and effort in our role or job, but at the same time, hanging on to something that doesn't deserve us because of our ego is also a waste.

---

[3]  Seth Godin, *The Dip* (Penguin Portfolio, 2007)

In his book he stated: 'At the beginning, when you first start something, it's fun. Over the next few days and weeks, the rapid learning you experience keeps you going. Whatever your new thing is, it's easy to stay engaged in it. And then the Dip happens. The Dip is the long slog between starting and mastery. I am sure most leaders can relate to this. Leader's block is a part of this dip.'

Once again, to know when to quit and when to stick requires a high level of self-awareness and that differentiates the good leaders from the great leaders.

## Proactive Feedback

Good leaders are constantly looking to improve and learn. One of the tools to do that is asking for feedback and inputs from those around you. Even though it may seem like a simple exercise, listening to others requires a high level of self-awareness.

In general, feedback is reactive; the person giving feedback always refers to incidents and behaviour that happened in the past. Here the emphasis is on being proactive, seeking feedback on an almost real-time basis. For example, asking a trusted adviser to observe you in a team meeting and then give their inputs and comments.

Asking for feedback is the first step. Digesting it, understanding it and then acting on it is the actual work. However, the key is selecting the people you are asking. They have to be part of your close circle (or inner circle), people you trust, people who know you well and will be honest with you. These inputs help you to stay grounded and close to reality because as leaders, it is very easy to become removed from reality.

I recall from my days in GE Capital, India, the head of the company, Pramod Bhasin, would always be in the cafeteria during lunchtime, sitting at different tables each day to speak with people in informal settings and thus getting to know the general mood of the organization. At times people wouldn't even realize that the CEO was sitting with them. It was his way of collecting input and feedback on what was working and what was not within the organization.

Several leaders that I know use similar methods to get informal and regular inputs, such as off-site meetings, post-work coffee, drinks or dinner.

Marshall Goldsmith coined a term that is now popular in the field of management and behaviour change. The term is 'feed-forward', meaning suggestions for the future. This is a concept that I use extensively in my coaching practice as I am certified on this methodology. This is how it works—instead of asking for feedback, the leaders ask their stakeholders for suggestions on what they can do differently in the future. So the approach is proactive, non-threatening and collaborative. The person giving suggestions doesn't feel any pressure and the receiver gets ideas for the future.

Sometimes it is not only about asking for feedback or 'feed-forward' but about being perceptive to those around you, such as your teams, your colleagues, your manager and even your close friends and family, picking up signals and clues from their narratives, body language and their reactions and responses to you. This will help you spot any change that people are seeing in you. It's about keeping your eyes and ears open!

## Philosophy of Flow

This is one of my favourite practices, something that I have been following consciously for the last couple of years. When you are in the flow it's difficult to be blocked. If you continue to keep yourself in the flow through practice, you can prevent leader's block.

According to Hungarian psychologist Mihaly Csikszentmihalyi, 'When we are deeply involved in trying to reach a goal, or an activity that is challenging but well-suited to our skills, we experience a joyful state called 'flow'.[4] One may find still greater happiness experiencing 'flow' in working towards long-term, meaningful goals.'

There are some easy ways to get into the flow. Keep aside at least an hour every day for 'uninterrupted creation time'. Avoid interruptions such as emails, social media or phone calls. There is enough research to show that multitasking is a big deterrent to getting into the flow. Do work that requires you to immerse yourself, such as reading, writing or solving a crossword or Sudoku. These activities are conducive to flow. The more you do these activities, the more easily you can create the flow at other times. The key is to keep practicing.

I am now in the habit of ensuring that I have no interruptions for two hours every morning (9.30–11.30 a.m.). I don't take any calls or schedule any meetings during that time. In fact, I used this time for writing this book, and before that I would use the time for reading or creating content for my keynote speeches. Initially, I would consciously practice getting into the flow by listening to music,

---

[4] Mihaly Csikszentmihalyi recognized and named the psychological concept of Flow, a highly focused mental state. He is distinguished professor of psychology and management at Claremont Graduate University, USA.

and at times it could take me almost an hour, but now it's easier for me. It's about doing it consistently.

## Board of Advisers

It is important to have a group of people who can serve as your sounding board. They can be your sponsor, mentor, colleagues or your coach. These are the people whom you should constantly talk to, not only when you are stuck. These are people who support you and provide the comradery that becomes harder to find as you become more senior.

One leader calls this group her 'personal board of advisers' and in it she has a diverse range of people from different age groups, different parts and periods of her life, and different backgrounds. The board includes her twenty-two-year-old son, her close friends from school and college, her ex-bosses, mentors, sponsors and her coach. She said there is one thing that they have in common and that is the only criteria to be on that board. These are people who don't judge her and are all brutally honest.

Another practical piece of advice from one of the global operating leaders of a service company was to talk to people who are radically different from you or those who have different backgrounds and experience. Doing this provides an outside-in view.

Some of the best advice and wisdom-filled nuggets I have received are from a friend who is an investment banker-turned-entrepreneur. He has a very different worldview, very different approach from mine, and yet it makes so much sense to me.

I would encourage leaders to put together their own board of advisers, and equally important is to make sure that it is diverse and that you are getting a good dose of outside-in perspectives. Just as an organization brings in external consultants to look at their problems or issues, it's good to have an external person look at our situation with a fresh set of eyes.

Another advantage of the board is that you have different people playing different roles. For example, a sponsor will ensure you get the right visibility, while a mentor will guide you based on their experience and a coach will help you in your self-awareness journey. Each role is important and has its relevance, therefore, the key is to have someone to fulfil each of them. If you have a problem or an issue that is troubling you, talk about it to this group. Share your concerns and express your opinion; sometimes speaking about it is half the battle won. Keeping things to ourselves, or letting them simmer inside us is not a healthy habit and a one-track road to leader's block.

I want to highlight the roles of family and friends here as they are the first ones to pick up on any changes in you and your behaviour, and also the first ones to be impacted. These are people who love you and support you unconditionally and therefore should be your constant source of advice and input.

## Early Warning Signs

Build self-awareness to recognize the early symptoms of leader's block. If you are getting bored, missing the spring in your feet, or the Monday morning blues continue for more than a few days, or you find that you are irritable and short-tempered for a few consecutive days, don't ignore it!

For me, when I start shouting at and getting impatient with my kids for small things, it is a reflection and manifestation of what is happening inside me. I know something is brewing. In fact, my children also know that something is wrong!

We know ourselves well and can see and feel any deviation in our behaviour, but the difficult part is to acknowledge it. *It can't happen to me, I am the leader.* That's the story we tell ourselves and therefore find it hard to accept and acknowledge that something is wrong. Many of the leaders I spoke to said that one of their key learnings from having experienced leader's block was to listen to their instincts as soon as they felt that something was wrong. They all had a hunch or intuition, but their logical mind took its time to accept it. A few of them said that if they had caught it earlier, the duration of the dilemma and pain would definitely have been less.

One of the ways to catch the early signs is to have greater self-awareness and that comes from being attuned to oneself, being aware of emotions and triggers. When you are self-aware you are in control, you decide where you want to focus your energy and emotions and that allows you to change behaviour and your mindset if you are not getting the results you want. When we are grounded, we are more focused and have the ability to control our minds, emotions and hence, our actions.

Self-awareness was conceived in the early '70s by Duval and Wicklund in their book *A Theory of Objective Self-Awareness*.[5] These are some of the actions that can help build greater self-awareness:

a. Have an open mind and be receptive to new ideas, new thoughts and new people.
b. Know your strengths and weaknesses so that you can leverage them accordingly.

---

[5] Robert Wicklund and Shelley Duval, *A Theory of Objective Self-Awareness* (Academic Press, 1972).

c. Recognize your emotional triggers, what's causing them and their impact.

d. Build self-discipline at work and in other areas of your life.

As I reflect on my own journey, after I overcame my leader's block in 2007, there were two more instances when I found myself blocked. One was while transitioning into a new role as a client relationship manager in the US and the other was when I worked with a manager whose operating style was drastically different from mine. These two instances were different from the first one in terms of their intensity and duration, but that was not by design, it was a stroke of luck. Coincidently, my mentor became my manager in the US, which eased my transition process. In the case of misalignment with my manager, before things started to impact me, my pregnancy came to the rescue and I went on a maternity break after working with him for about six months. I then came back to a new role.

If I had had the awareness and knowledge that I have today, I could have prevented those instances or recognized the symptoms earlier and reached out for help. I wish this book had been available to me then!

It is often said that leadership is a marathon and not a sprint and therefore leaders need to build enough endurance and stamina to last. One of the ways to build endurance is to recognize the possible obstacles and learn how to overcome them. One of those major obstacles is leader's block, which every leader will encounter and eventually overcome, some faster and less painfully than others. But if it is ignored then the leaders may derail or burnout and not complete the marathon. The key is to prevent that obstacle from recurring or be able to foresee it and take proactive action. It's imperative to cultivate practices in our daily lives that can help us recognize the symptoms much earlier, acknowledge them and address them. Over time, this awareness will help in building immunity.

Like most things in life, there is no one set formula or one practice; we all need to find our own formula—the one that works for us, our situation and our requirements. As you have read, most of these practices, if not all, require a high level of self-awareness, self-discipline and self-reflection.

Which of these preventive practices are you engaging in to build immunity so that you can foresee and anticipate any obstacle before it becomes a leader's block?

a. Are you keeping aside some time to reflect daily?
b. Are you proactively collecting inputs from people who matter?
c. Are you pursuing a hobby or vocation?
d. Are you doing something to learn constantly?
e. Do you practice any activity that gets you into the flow?

> The most potent preventive for leader's block is to regularly step back, reflect and plan ahead.

# 8

# Role of the Organization

Organizations can play an important and active role not only in helping leaders recognize, acknowledge and overcome leader's block, but also in creating awareness about it. Before we discuss the how, I want us to understand and clarify the meaning of an organization. Here are three common definitions:

a. An organized group of people with a particular purpose, such as a business or government department.
b. A social unit of people that is structured and managed to meet a need or to pursue collective goals.

c. An organization in its simplest form is a person or group of people intentionally organized to accomplish an overall, common goal or set of goals.

These definitions make it clear that an organization is not a stand-alone entity; it is a group of people. Often I hear people talking about the organization as if it is a separate entity. For example, they will say things such as 'the culture in our organization is bureaucratic', or 'the values of my company resonate with me', or 'our organization allows us enough flexibility', whereas they are actually referring to the leadership team, to the decision makers.

An organization is the sum of its people, its culture, its environment, its values, its brand, its ways of working, all of which are defined by people. These people could be the founders (if it is a start-up), the board, CEOs and their teams, the HR team, the teams that are decision makers, the people who lead teams, and essentially anyone who impacts the people in the company.

In the rest of the chapter, when I use the term 'organization' I am referring to its leaders and the decision makers.

The theme of the book, 'for the leader from the leader', continues and hence it is important for the organization (read for the leaders) to understand what leader's block is and how they may be playing a role, consciously or unconsciously, in causing it, and equally important, what role they can play in helping leaders overcome it.

One of the first things that the organization can do is to remove the taboo or stigma attached to this phase. All the leaders I interviewed wanted to remain anonymous. One of the reasons for this was that they did not want to share their perceived failure openly and publicly. Some of them also mentioned that they were reluctant about people in their office knowing about this phase as they felt they would be judged; the temporary phase could even have repercussions on their appraisal and reputation.

One of my biggest insights from interviewing leaders was that despite leader's block being so common, people didn't feel comfortable talking about it; they had a fear of judgment. 'I am a seasoned leader so how can I be experiencing this?' They thought they were the only ones to experience a leader's block and that there was something wrong with them if they were experiencing it. When I shared with these leaders that they were not alone and that there were many leaders who had experienced leader's block, they all felt a huge sense of relief!

Their concerns are not unfounded because organizations and our society don't allow leaders to fail—even if it's temporary. We expect our leaders to be perfect and larger-than-life characters like Superman and Wonder Woman. There is a lot of pressure on them. For example, a leader is expected to be competent and yet be open to new education; be a servant leader and also set direction for the team; be authentic yet build a strong presence; be responsible and also delegate; be resilient yet vulnerable; be extraordinary yet humble, and the list goes on. Organizations need to realize and tell their leaders that it is not possible to perform at their best all the time, and that's all right.

Brene Brown's TED Talk, 'Listening to Shame', is one of my favourite talks. She talks about being vulnerable and defines vulnerability as 'the accurate definition of courage'. That is a powerful insight as it does take a lot of courage to acknowledge our shortcomings and failures. It is true—in our corporate world there is so much shame attached to leaders who don't do well. Admitting to experiencing leader's block makes them feel ashamed, that they have failed as leaders, and they start to self-doubt and lose confidence, so naturally, they don't talk about it.

We expect our leaders to learn new things or get better at what they do—be more creative, be more authentic, be more charismatic, be more assertive—

but often we overlook what they want or what they are struggling with. We rarely talk about the things or blocks that may be tripping them up, that may be stopping them from moving forward. This conversation has to start from the top.

Giving this phase a name—leader's block—is the first step in enabling more open conversations. Organizations need to encourage more open dialogue in team and one-on-one meetings where leaders can talk and share what they are going through and how they are coping with it, so that people can learn from each other. Facilitating and urging open discussions is the first step in removing the taboo or stigma attached to leader's block.

When Sheryl Sandberg started the Lean In[1] circles, the intention was to create a platform for women to start talking and sharing their issues. By doing so it opened up the dialogue on discovering solutions that were unique to women, along with how women could support and learn from each other. I wonder if we can create something similar for leaders. A place where leaders can come together and talk about their challenges openly. Most of the conferences and workshops are either about subject matter expertise or leadership—how

---

[1] Sherly Sandberg, *Lean In* (Alfred A. Knopf, 2013).

to be better at what you do or how to be a great leader. There aren't any conferences that enable or encourage us to speak about the challenges that leaders go through. When I asked the leaders I spoke to, almost all of them said that they wished there was a forum where they could talk, share and learn from each other openly.

Typically, organizations invest in areas where they can show a clear return on investment, where there is a metric that can show improvement, or in things that are topical. For example, these days the focus is on diversity and inclusion. I do not doubt or question the movement, in fact being a woman I am a big supporter, but my point is that at times organizations ignore things or areas that can't be clearly measured or those that are not so comfortable to talk about. Brene Brown said that when corporates book her to give a talk, they often ask her not to talk about 'shame' and 'vulnerability'. This validates my point that we don't want to talk about things that make us appear weak.

We have read about the impact of leader's block on the organization, its culture and its environment. Organizations would have to be naïve to ignore leader's block, its existence and its effect. They cannot close their eyes and wish the issue of leader's block away.

According to a *Harvard Business Review*[2] article published in July 2018, Deloitte surveyed 1000 full-time employees in the US and found that 77 per cent had experienced burnout at their current jobs, and more than half said they'd felt it more than once. This was true even though 87 per cent of respondents said they 'have passion for their job'. At the same time, nearly seven in ten people (69 per cent) said they feel their employer 'does not do enough to minimize burnout'. While these numbers are specific to the US, based on my interviews with leaders across the globe, these numbers can be extrapolated globally without much variation. These are alarming statistics!

As leader's block is a precursor to a burnout, organizations have a huge opportunity to prevent burnout by helping leaders identify and overcome leader's block.

As a global keynote speaker, when I share my own example of leader's block and ask the audience to raise their hands if my story resonates with them, or if they have experienced something similar, almost everyone in the room raises their hand. To encourage

---

[2] Matt Plummer, 'How Are You Protecting Your High Performers from Burnout?' *Harvard Business Review* (June 2018).

them to share and get over their reluctance, I ask the audience members to have a quick discussion with the person sitting next to them. Similarly, when I introduce the topic of leader's block to a smaller group and start by sharing my story, it always leads to a great conversation. Leaders start sharing with each other and there is a sense of belonging or comradery. Organizations need more of these conversations. We need to talk more about leader's block. As leaders we will set the tone for our teams and create a culture of more honest communication.

When I asked leaders whether organizations could do something to help them during this phase, all of them answered with a resounding yes. One leader pointed out that organizations need to acknowledge that some of their senior leaders will go through this temporary phase, and that doesn't make the leader less desirable. There isn't enough awareness about these blocks and there isn't enough dialogue that explains that everyone might experience these patches, that they are temporary and that you get through them with some interventions.

For an organization to raise awareness on leader's block, it needs to be familiar with the symptoms. There is no science to recognizing it; the organization just needs to pay more attention to its leaders, to their narrative, behaviour, body language, engagement, mood and temperament rather than looking only at the metrics, targets and results.

If you recall the reasons that trigger leader's block, most of them are driven by the organization, whether it is ignoring the fact that a leader has been doing the same role for X number of years, or overlooking the quality of supervisors because they may be bringing in good business for the organization, or not investing enough in a leader when they are transitioning into a new role.

Organizations can be more deliberate about the duration of time leaders spend in a role. They could help find a balance between gaining expertise by spending time in a role, and intellectual and mental stimulation for the leader. Also, the organization should recognize that each leader is unique. For some, spending five years in a job provides stability while for others, boredom sets in after three years. Many organizations have a job rotation policy, but the key is effectiveness—one blanket policy may not work for all leaders. The other aspect is job suitability. Even if leaders are rotated, do they get the jobs that they are the best fit for? For example, one leader could perform well in a particular role but could be a misfit for another, so finding the sweet spot of each leader and leveraging their skills is important. For example, placing a business development person in data analytics or asking the strategy head to run operations may not work without some mentoring and coaching.

At the same time, organizations are required to create new opportunities for their leaders. Organizations need to take more risks with their people, be more intentional about providing them roles that may not be directly related to their experience, but are roles that the leader has the potential to do and will be enthusiastic about. Organizations can give leaders additional responsibilities or projects to optimize their potential.

In Wendy's case, when the role fatigue had set in, she spoke to her manager about it. Once they had clarity on what she wanted to do, the organization provided her the opportunity to get involved in a global project that suited her skill set and didn't jeopardize her existing role. It became a win-win situation.

Some of the larger and more successful organizations today have stringent hiring processes. But once the crème de la crème are hired, they don't necessarily get the roles that utilize their full potential. One of the leaders in a major technology company shared that the majority of the leaders around him, including himself, were performing below their actual potential and that it was just a matter of time before more leaders started to get blocked, if they weren't already blocked.

It is a huge change for leaders when they transition into a new role, new domain or even a new geography. I was surprised to find that very few organizations even have a transition plan, let alone a robust one. This is an area that leaders at all levels struggle with, but more so at senior levels. For junior levels, most organizations have a checklist and a handover document for tactical processes. At senior levels there is a clear gap; leaders are expected to figure things out on their own, which could be overwhelming in a complex situation.

A *Harvard Business Review*[3] article published in July 2018 talks about the transition process for CEOs. According to the article, Egon Zehnder, a leadership development firm, surveyed 402 CEOs from eleven countries, and 68 per cent of them said that they were not ready for the job! They were ready on the strategic and business aspects of their roles, but less prepared for the personal and interpersonal part of leadership. I am sure that if we were to use the same survey for senior leaders who are transitioning into big roles the result won't be very different. One of the downsides of not being

---

[3]  Cassandra Frangos, *Harvard Business Review* (July 2018).

prepared is that it can quickly become leader's block. Therefore, organizations need to prepare and support their leaders in advance.

Nancy, who had struggled with transitioning and her two warring managers, shared that as she looks back, she wishes that the organization had supported her better. She lamented the fact that she didn't ask for a mentor or a coach to help her through that phase. If you recall, she said that was the loneliest period of her career.

Similarly, Malti's example of transitioning into a step-up role without much support from the organization is a case in point where organizations could be more intentional, more planned.

As leaders become more senior they don't always ask for help and don't know whom to ask for help without being judged, as they are expected to know it all. This dilemma puts them in a tough spot. During transitions, one part is about the structure and the process, and the other is about the mindset. Transitioning to step-up roles requires a mindset change, which can be worked through with an external coach or active mentoring as most of the time it is about helping the leader build more self-confidence.

For leaders looking for structure and guidance, I would recommend the classic book on transitions,

*The First 90 Days*,[4] by Michael Watkins. It is an excellent guide for leaders transitioning into new roles as it lays down the strategy for making an impact in the first ninety days of your new role or job. In my coaching engagements, I use this framework when I am helping leaders prepare for transitions.

The quality of supervisors is another common factor that triggers leader's block, and as we read in Frank's case, even the most seasoned leaders are impacted if their supervisor is not supportive. Even though a company's culture may be open, if the immediate manager is closed to new suggestions and ideas, the leader will not benefit from that culture. At times, organizations ignore or overlook this issue as that particular leader or leaders may be getting the business for the organization, or they may not want to disrupt an existing set-up.

In Elly's case, she waited for the organization to find out about her supervisor's behaviour and then acted on it, and that wait drove her to the brink of quitting. In most cases, managers are competent people; they are achievers, hence they are in that position, but it is their attitude that is detrimental to the team. Most organizations focus on results and the

---

[4] Michael Watkin, *The First 90 Days* (Harvard Business School Press, 2006).

managers get them the results; it is the interpersonal aspect that is ignored, which can have consequences such as leader's block. A shift is therefore required from 'what you achieve' to 'how you achieve'. Organizations need to take the required action even if it involves their senior leaders, because if they don't it sets the wrong precedent for others in the organization. There are also some systemic changes that organizations need to make to improve the quality of supervisors, such as creating a broader culture of coaching and mentoring.

Back in 2008, an internal team of researchers at Google launched Project Oxygen to determine what makes a manager great. They came up with a list of competencies, which is regularly updated. In 2018, out of the ten competencies, the number one was 'to be a good coach' and number three was 'showing concern for success and well-being', thus emphasizing the importance of a good supervisor and looking beyond numbers.

For senior leaders there is one more function that plays a big part in their success. That is the human resource partner (or HR partner as they are commonly called). The HR partner works closely with the leader and is often the first one to notice any changes in the leader's behaviour and attitude. HR partners should not be polite and pleasing, but rather challenging and questioning to help the leader recognize and acknowledge the patterns and symptoms of leader's block.

Another way that organizations can help leaders overcome and prevent leader's block is to provide them with external and internal support. Most of the leaders that I interviewed said that their organizations focused on leadership training and development at the junior and mid-levels but not at the senior levels. The assumption is that leaders know it all, and that is where the issues start. Things are changing so fast that what leaders learnt over the last ten to fifteen years of their career may not be relevant, not only for products and technology, but also for leadership and leadership styles.

Similarly, many organizations have a formal structured programme on mentoring, but again that is more focused on and targeted at mid-level management. Many senior leaders become mentors, but who mentors them? Who motivates the leader? Even a doctor has to consult a specialist when self-treatment doesn't work!

Organizations should encourage leaders to have executive coaches as leaders at the top need confidants and sounding boards. They need an outside-in view and also a psychological safety net. A coach brings an external perspective with no fear of judgment and can also challenge leaders by probing, questioning and even opposing their views. One could argue that this can be done by the leader's team and peers, but this doesn't happen often as there is a reluctance to challenge one's boss. Also, with one's colleagues, there are a lot of egos and insecurities at play. Everyone is trying to drive their agenda and so an outside perspective is neutral and insightful. Victor, the senior partner from a top audit firm, reiterated that it would have been so much easier if the partners had had coaches as they were going through the transition from audit team members to partners.

Apart from supporting leaders in overcoming and preventing leader's block, the organization plays a big role in creating awareness about leader's block. For them to create awareness they need to acknowledge its presence. When I talk to HR leaders about my research they like it and can relate to it, but in the same breath they also sheepishly acknowledge that if they checked with their leaders no one would admit to experiencing leader's block, at least officially. Ironically, these were conversations with the HR leaders of the same organizations whose leaders I have interviewed. This goes on to prove that acknowledging leader's block officially is the starting point for creating awareness.

I spoke to some experienced HR folks to find out if they were able to identify this temporary block, and it did appear that more often than not they could not diagnose it. To them it appeared to be a skill or will issue, which is often not the case. It is probably time to relook at the issue and start to talk about it more openly. HR folks are the best people to start the movement as they define the culture of an organization, which then becomes the norm and accepted behaviour across all levels. HR, along with the leadership team, plays a big role in setting the tone for the organization, and there is no better way to display that than to walk the talk. If the leadership sets the tone for being open and non-judgemental, the teams under them will follow suit.

I would like to see companies make leader's block a part of their accepted jargon. For example, if a leader says, 'I think I am going through a leader's block', his manager should reply, 'Well, you can go and speak with Joe, he overcame his block recently.' It is similar to when we are stuck with a work-related report or analysis. We ask someone for help, someone who has done it before or is an expert. We could do the same with leader's block!

Leader's block has to move from a closed door conversation to a corridor conversation. This doesn't require any big organizational change or structural change, it requires only a mindset change that is driven by leaders across all levels and is therefore embedded in the organization's culture. It may take a little time, but it is possible. When organizations look at the competencies and effectiveness of a leader, and if it appears that the leader hasn't gone through a leader's block, then there is something wrong there! It is akin to building muscle memory for resilience. If you haven't faced any challenges or blocks, are you really ready to lead? That is a question to ask. It is a prerequisite to being a great leader.

Another way to create awareness about leader's block is to build the ability to recognize its symptoms and the patterns of behaviour associated with it.

Once leaders go through a leader's block they can see it in others, which can help them mentor and coach new leaders about the block. In fact many leaders that I spoke with said that the fact that they had experienced leader's block made them more perceptive, so when they saw it in others, they were more empathetic and wanted to help as they knew what it felt like. HR and senior leaders should start talking about leader's block with emerging leaders and that is why it is important for managers to have the skill to be a coach. By being just a manager it might be difficult to catch leader's block as in most cases outward performance is not impacted. It's only when you start approaching it from a coaching perspective that you get a glimpse of what is really going on beneath the surface. Also, leaders acknowledging their own journey will help the teams under them to start opening up and sharing. It's about starting open conversations.

Through my book and my research I hope to spread the message that leader's block is not negative, it's not a failure and it's definitely not something to be ashamed of. My reasons for saying so are:

a. Leader's block is temporary. We can overcome it once we recognize and acknowledge it.
b. We come out of leader's block stronger, wiser and with more clarity. We get an opportunity to step back and look at our life holistically.
c. We are not alone. All great leaders go through it and come out of it, and I believe each one of us is a great leader.

While this chapter talks specifically about the role of the organization in helping leaders recognize and cope with leader's block, the organization plays an active role in the overall well-being of the employee. Progressive organizations go beyond providing high salaries and perks; they provide their leaders with a higher purpose and objective. They try to align the personal aspirations of the leaders to the purpose of the organization. They create an environment that allows leaders to follow their passion and hobbies without impacting their output. Great organizations make sure their top leaders lead by example, whether it's taking time off work regularly or not responding to emails during the weekend. These organizations go beyond hiring the best, they make their leaders the best by allowing them to fail and learn from their mistakes. We need more of these organizations for leaders to thrive in times of uncertainty and ambiguity.

We are in the age of technological disruption and though more and more jobs will be done by robots and artificial intelligence, the constant innovation and improvization can be done only by humans. How will any advancement happen if leaders themselves are blocked?

Organizations must encourage open dialogues to move leader's block from a closed room conversation to a corridor conversation.

# 9

# Thermometer for Leader's Block

Going back to the flu analogy, when we are coming down with the flu, we start to display certain symptoms. We get a cough, the sniffles, we carry a tissue with us and then we use a thermometer to measure our temperature.

Similarly, how do we know if we could be heading towards a leader's block or already have it? Let's find out by answering the following questions:

a. Are you finding yourself to be adrift and disengaged in meetings?
b. Are you browsing the Internet mindlessly for hours during your office hours?

c. Are you becoming more irritable and short-tempered?

d. Are you working harder than usual and yet not making progress?

e. Are you becoming very task-oriented and micromanaging your team?

f. Are you avoiding new initiatives and not pushing the envelope enough?

g. Are you sounding cynical and negative, and do you say things such as 'this is done like this only', or 'I don't think this will work'?

h. Are you less engaged and increasingly bored at work?

i. Are you missing the bounce in your feet?

j. Are you experiencing the Monday morning blues every day of the week?

**Green:** If you said 'yes' to less than three questions, your temperature range is 98.6–99° Fahrenheit. You are fine; continue doing what you are doing.

**Yellow:** If you said 'yes' to three to five questions, your temperature range is 99–100° Fahrenheit. You might be getting that cold and cough, so watch it closely.

**Red:** If you said 'yes' to more than five questions, your temperature is above 100° Fahrenheit. You definitely have the flu. It's time to see a doctor.

For a detailed diagnostic, complete the leader's block assessment at www.leadersblock.com.

# 10

# Leaders in Action

This section of the book contains examples and incidents that bring to life all the key points that we have discussed so far. These stories are of leaders like you and me.

I have selected these narratives to depict the diversity, uniqueness and breadth of the types of leaders, organizations, situations and solutions. I am sure you will be able to relate to them directly or indirectly.

The purpose of these anecdotes is not to highlight how great these leaders are, although they are. The purpose is to emphasize and show the human side of these leaders, their mistakes, their fears, their failures and their blocks, and to learn how they overcame them.

None of these leaders had magic or a superpower to overcome their challenges, but they all had the self-awareness to step back and reflect, the courage to acknowledge their failure and the modesty to ask for help. For me, these leaders represent the unsung heroes of the corporate world.

I hope you will enjoy and learn by reading these stories as much as I enjoyed and learnt by listening to them.

*These stories are of the leaders I have interviewed and coached. Their names and the names of their organizations have been changed to protect their privacy.*

## The PowerPoint

Rhea was a successful leader who had held large operating roles in a global professional services company. She had excellent people management skills; her customers, both internal and external, loved her. She was passionate about her work and was well respected by her peers and subordinates alike. She was well networked and enjoyed good equity as she had been with the organization for ten years.

A few months back, she went for her maternity break. When she returned, she applied for a job in a new function within the organization. The job looked very interesting; it was a role that she hadn't done before so it provided a great opportunity for her to learn.

The organization had brought in Gianni, an external hire, to lead the new function. Gianni came with a wealth of experience in working with top-notch consulting firms, which gave him an edge within the organization. He was excited about setting up the new function and had great plans to make it a success. When Gianni interviewed Rhea, he instantly liked her personality and her willingness to learn. He was impressed by her management experience and communication style, though he did notice that she had not done any consulting roles before. That was the only negative, but he went ahead and hired her.

Rhea was excited to join the function and soon the team grew to six members. Apart from Rhea, Gianni had hired the rest of the team from consulting firms, but she was the most senior, not only in terms of her years of experience but also in designation.

The first three months were great. Rhea loved the way Gianni structured his ideas and thoughts, she found his consulting style refreshing, and she was learning a lot. Gianni knew that Rhea had a strong internal network and was a great communicator. He was looking for her to be the ambassador of the team internally. They both had very distinct and almost opposite operating styles. Rhea loved free-flowing discussion and the exchange of ideas, she enjoyed working with people to get things done rather than sitting behind the desk and doing it herself. Gianni on the other hand was very structured; he never met anyone if it wasn't scheduled in his calendar and spent the entire day at his desk researching and documenting his ideas. He even ate at his desk.

The honeymoon was soon over and slowly their different styles started to clash. They were falling short on each other's expectations. Gianni came from a background where 'the deck' (aka the PowerPoint) was the end product of all efforts; clients paid millions of dollars to consulting firms for that final twenty-page deck. Rhea on the other hand was all about managing and getting work done by her teams across the globe. According to her, the deck was best left to the sales people. Also for her, it was how you said it rather than what you said.

Gianni's vision was to operate the team like a consulting firm. He wanted the team to be very structured and have high quality standards, especially in producing PowerPoints since they were reflective of the work the team did. It worked for the rest of the team since they came from a consulting environment, but not for Rhea.

Gianni was a progressive leader; when he started to notice the friction between Rhea and himself, he brought in an executive coach, and that's how I know this story!

When I came on board, I met with Gianni to get his input and feedback on Rhea. He said he really liked Rhea's positive attitude and leadership style and was fond of her as a person. He felt that her level of engagement was declining, and I asked him why he felt that. He said that it reflected in the decks that she sent him. He felt that her attention to detail wasn't up to his standards and thought it could be intentional as he had given her detailed and specific feedback a few times. After an hour of conversation with Gianni, I walked out of the room with the insight that Gianni's peeve with Rhea was the deck.

My first meeting with Rhea was quite interesting. Contrary to what Gianni had said, Rhea didn't seem to have a positive attitude. She came to that meeting as if it was an obligation. Later in the conversation, she mentioned that she thought getting a coach was Gianni's way of managing her. That rang a bell for me. She hadn't been involved in the decision to get a coach and moreover she had had no proper briefing on why she was getting a coach. Despite his good intentions, Gianni had missed communicating effectively. This is where organizations go wrong—

in the positioning of coaching to their employees. I told Rhea that only if she felt comfortable with me should she continue.

A week after our initial meeting, she and I had our first session. I learnt about her background and the previous roles she had performed. She had an impressive trajectory in the organization. She was one of the youngest vice presidents in the company and had done some great international assignments. She did indeed have a personable and likeable demeanour. However, what caught my attention was that despite all the success behind her, she didn't appear very confident and assured. As I started asking her about her current role she began opening up. She told me that she had taken on the role, which was completely outside of what she had done before, as she had wanted to learn and challenge herself. After nine months in the role, she thought she was a failure. I asked her what made her think that and she said that she couldn't produce good PowerPoints. She said this in all seriousness.

What seemed like a minor or innocuous thing was more than that. Rhea was not able to understand Gianni's obsession with PowerPoints. She had initially enjoyed her meetings and interactions with him as he would talk about new ideas and products, but slowly those conversations started to become more tactical and detailed. Rhea's strengths were ideation, guiding people to do things and marketing her function within the organization. That's what she had been hired for, or at least that's what she had thought. She found herself in a situation where Gianni expected her to deliver on something she wasn't interested in and wasn't her core skill or strength.

The typical interaction cycle was that Gianni would ask Rhea to prepare a deck and Rhea would put in her best, but somehow that wouldn't match Gianni's standards. He would think she had intentionally not put in much effort, so he would send her a detailed note with his feedback. Rhea dreaded reading those emails, and hence the cycle of mistrust and micromanagement would perpetuate. She said those emails were so caustic, and almost insulting, that they shook her confidence. She wasn't able to meet Gianni's standards even though she tried her best. She was demotivated and uninspired; she withdrew and stopped interacting with her colleagues. She wasn't herself and it happened so subtly that it took her time to realize it, but soon others around her started to notice the changes. She was no longer her positive and bright self. She was in the middle of a classic leader's block.

From our conversations one thing was clear, it was not the PowerPoint that was the main issue.

It was the lack of trust between Gianni and Rhea, and that stemmed from the fact that both had very different skill sets and expectations from each other. It was a case of misalignment of skills with the job requirement, coupled with very distinct or contrasting personalities.

Since Rhea was demoralized she had slowly started to become disengaged in meetings and her involvement in the team started to drop. This was perceived as almost defiance by Gianni so he started to be more critical in his feedback and micromanaging more. Both Rhea and Gianni were mature leaders and you would expect them to sit and talk and sort it out, but sometimes the obvious is difficult to see or do.

As you can see, the simple solution to this issue would have been that both leaders recognized each other's strengths and leveraged them. Gianni should have realized Rhea's strengths and used them to build relationships and networks for his group. He should have let her run the function while he could have focused on the research, analysis and the decks. Similarly, Rhea should have put in more effort or showed more interest in learning a new skill.

Since I knew both sides of the story, I got them to set up a session to talk openly and give each other feedback, but that didn't go anywhere as it became a one-sided conversation. Rhea could not muster the courage to tell Gianni about her dislike for working behind the desk and how she was trying to do her best to make better PowerPoints. This lack of communication didn't help the cause. In the first annual appraisal Rhea was rated 'meets expectations', a rating she had never received in the ten years she had been with the organization. She had always been rated 'exceeds expectation'.

The story didn't have the expected happy ending despite my best efforts. After a few months, Rhea applied for another internal job and moved on. Our sessions did help her regain her confidence once she realized that it was better for her to leverage and grow her existing strengths rather than work on an area where she would always be average. Gianni accepted that he was not able to do justice to Rhea's talent and reluctantly let her go. He continued to grow the function and did very well.

As you reflect on this study, you will understand that there is no right or wrong. These were leaders with two different styles struggling to work with each other. However, there are things that they could have done differently.

One of the key responsibilities of a manager is to develop and nurture talent. In this case Gianni could have realized Rhea's strengths much earlier and also acknowledged the fact that she came from a very different background. He could have been more open and transparent with her in terms of sharing the bigger picture, his perspective and thoughts behind the final outcome of the PowerPoint. While he did all the right things on paper, his actions weren't congruent all the time. He could have communicated better. For example, he hired a coach for Rhea with the intention of helping her, but not only did he not communicate this to her, but he also wanted to drive the results in his favour.

While managers have a big role to play, I also think that as a senior leader Rhea could have managed the situation better. For example, she could have reached out to some of her mentors in her network for their advice. She could have had an open dialogue with Gianni and explained her situation rather than ignoring it. She could have taken more interest in learning to make better PowerPoint decks, or she could have found some external help to do that. She could have found a way around the issue rather than giving up.

In this case there were two things that stood out for me. The first was the positioning of coaching within the organization. When I came on board, Rhea was sceptical, whereas it was an investment as she was a high potential leader. Secondly, I got the sense that the culture wasn't conducive to open communication, and maybe that was why Rhea wasn't able to share her predicament with Gianni.

This seems to be a straightforward issue that should have been easy to resolve. But humans are complex beings and at the heart of all the issues is lack of trust, and one of the ways to build it is through open communication.

I am in contact with both Gianni and Rhea and they are both doing well in their careers. Different things work for different personalities. The key is to recognize the issues and work around them.

## The Golden Handcuffs

For Matt, it was a dream come true. After multiple gruelling interviews, he had finally made it to the company of his dreams. He had been a bundle of nerves throughout the month-long hiring process, as he had read that this company received almost two million job applications every year and less than 0.05 per cent of the applicants were hired. Going by that number, his was no small feat. He was on top of the world and felt like he was the crème de la crème.

He joined the organization with a lot of enthusiasm, excitement and pride. His prior experience was with two top-level technology firms. He had a degree from an Ivy League college and had always been a super achiever. The added joy was that he had recently moved back to his home country, China.

On his first day in the office, Matt learnt that the person who had hired him would soon be leaving. That person's role had changed and all the people whom he had hired had to find roles in other divisions. Matt started in a role that was quite different from the one he had been hired for. He wanted to run a business, but in reality he was running a very small team of product specialists supporting the sales team. He didn't mind as it was a new industry and a new market, and he enjoyed the environment. He did the role for about two years, then applied for another job within the company and moved to Singapore. Again, this second role didn't completely match his potential, but it was an Asia-Pacific role, so he was looking after a bigger territory. He did that role for about two and a half years.

It wasn't until the third role that Matt felt he was doing something that matched his potential and stretched his intellect. His new role involved three different teams, multiple products and big target numbers to achieve. It was tough, but he felt he was ready for it after the previous five years of underperforming. Matt felt his new role was a perfect fit for his skill and knowledge. The role was complex and the first six months were intense.

It had taken Matt five years to reach this role and it was challenging him. He was constantly thinking. He felt he was operating at a different level mentally and physically as compared to his last two roles. Matt went on to build and grow the business from $500 million to $4 billion over a period of five years and was very proud of his achievement. But he also started to realize that his learning curve was plateauing.

When I met Matt, he was on a short sabbatical and was about to start a new job with a start-up. I was intrigued by his story. The organization he was leaving was his dream company and he had done fairly well there. After all, he was the crème de la crème of the industry. I wanted to know more.

He told me that his disappointment had started when he didn't get the role he had been hired for. He had felt a little betrayed, but he also knew that his situation was not uncommon. His move to Singapore was to get away from his first role, even though he knew that the new role wasn't what he wanted to do. Slowly, as he built his network, he started to learn that he wasn't alone. There were many people like him who weren't happy with the roles they were doing, but the allure of great perks, a great environment and the sense of pride in being attached to the organization kept them going. It disturbed him a little, but he didn't pay much attention to it.

It was not until his third role that he realized that the problem of people being underutilized was rampant. In this role he had to build a team and that meant hiring people. Most of the resumés he received were from internal candidates. As he went through them he realized that the majority of them were doing a job that was below their potential and experience. They were overqualified for the roles that they were doing and interviewing for.

The organization had great people practices in place, coaching and mentoring was embedded in their culture, there was a lot of focus on personal development and skill development and that was the biggest attraction for people, along with the biggest retention strategy. However, as humans we always want more, we are constantly looking for progress and unless we continue to learn and contribute we cannot progress.

Going back to Matt's example, his third role finally stretched him and gave him an opportunity to learn and contribute to the business. He was very happy doing what he was doing until he hit the five-year mark and his learning stopped. He started to get into autopilot mode. He could do the job with 5 per cent of his brain capacity. He had built a strong team that could manage most of the work. He got involved with some initiatives, but it was a temporary fix. He began to spend more time in the gym and the cafeteria than in his office, and the elements of the job that had attracted him previously had lost their charm.

Matt finally decided to speak to his manager and told him that he wanted to look for another role. His manager was supportive and agreed. So began his search to find a good role for himself internally. With gusto he started to follow the internal job postings. He wanted to make sure that this time he took on a role that not only matched his potential but also helped him get to the next level in the organization. He wanted to take his time and was in no hurry. He was also open to relocating.

Matt soon realized that open positions for senior roles were quite limited. Weeks passed by and after three months he had not found a suitable role. Meanwhile, his current job was being managed well by his team leader and was fast becoming self-managed. He got involved only when there were escalations, which were few. Matt found himself in the bizarre position of not being needed by his existing team and not having a new role either.

Matt described this period as one of the hardest of his career. His self-esteem, self-confidence, self-respect—everything took a hit. He started to doubt himself and couldn't fathom how he had managed to get there. He was experiencing a leader's block—he was not able to perform at his best.

He decided to lower his expectations and started to apply for roles he had initially decided against. He applied for four internal jobs. He received requests to interview for all of them. For two of those roles the interviewing manager found him overqualified and advised him against taking it; Matt agreed. Finally, after a month of back and forth regarding the other two roles, Matt took up one. It wasn't very exciting, but Matt was tired of trying and being without a proper job. He said that he talked himself into believing that he was going to make it work and tried to be positive.

I was curious. I asked him why he didn't think of leaving the organization and looking for a job outside. He smiled and said, 'Golden handcuffs'.

Matt spoke to his friends and peers at work about his situation and they all told him that he was doing well, and that it was up to him to make something out of the role. They tried to give him comfort by saying that they were also not necessarily doing roles that aligned with their potential and interests. Matt shared that this fact didn't comfort him, it bothered him.

Nonetheless, he started his new role on a positive note. Every morning on his way to work he would listen to podcasts and interviews to motivate and energize himself. He wanted to make a positive impact on his new team and new manager. He learnt his new role very quickly and became good at it, but something didn't feel right. His heart wasn't there. Even though he had tried hard, he found himself becoming disengaged quickly. He performed the role for eighteen months until he decided to take some action.

He finally called it quits. As Matt told me his story, I asked what took him so long to make that decision and he again said, 'Golden handcuffs'. He explained that in this case it wasn't just financial but also all the other paraphernalia. I asked him to explain. He proceeded to tell me that every time he had thought of leaving, the first thing that came to his mind was that he was working for his dream company, and that he had worked very hard to get there. He couldn't see how he could just let it go. His dilemma received similar reactions from the people around him. They reiterated the fact that he must not leave the organization. The organization had the environment, perks and facilities that he found very difficult to walk away from. Where else could he find the same flexi hours, the work ethic, the development programmes, the peer group? These were the questions that came to his mind when he thought of leaving. He was scared that he would find it difficult to adjust in any other company.

Matt is not alone in this. There are many others like him who find themselves in similar situations where they feel underutilized and yet are unable to leave easily. To me this is a perfect combination to foster leader's block—not being able to perform at your best and yet continuing to perpetuate that.

Matt said that, upon reflection, he knew he should have left when he was not able to find a good job-fit internally. He had put himself through the additional misery of eighteen months by taking up the last role. He wished he had recognized and acknowledged that he was going through a leader's block as that would have helped him overcome it faster.

In this case I think the organization had a big role to play. They had done the right thing by creating an environment conducive to learning. They had provided all manner of perks and benefits for their employees, but the key point that they had missed was utilizing their employees to their fullest potential. They overlooked the fact that every person is looking for constant growth and progress. This situation is detrimental not only to the employees but also to the organization as a big percentage of their people can get into a leader's block if they find themselves underutilized. And that would result in unproductivity and attrition.

In Matt's case they could have enhanced his job or given him additional responsibilities or involved in a company-wide initiative. They should have found avenues to utilize his talent and knowledge instead of letting it go to waste. If you were to add up all the Matts in the organization, imagine the amount of brain power and capacity that is being wasted.

In April 2018, *Business Insider*[1] published an article about retention in new age technology firms such as Google, Facebook, Uber, Dropbox, Tesla, Airbnb, Netflix, Salesforce and others, which validates my point. The average tenure of employees in these firms is two to three years, in spite of all the perks and benefits. So what are they missing?

They are missing the unleashing of the true potential of their people.

## Hot Potato

Amit was still in shock as he walked back to his room after his meeting with Cindy, the head of HR. He put his feet up on the desk and shut his eyes. He still remembered his first day in this company vividly. It seemed the years since had gone by in a flash. As he

---

[1] Article by *Business Insider*, USA published in 2018 by Kaylee Fagan

looked back, he realized so much had happened in the last five years.

Amit had joined an insurance mammoth after spending fifteen years in a bank and was hired as the strategy head for the Europe, Middle East and Africa (EMEA) markets. He was a subject matter expert on strategy and knew that he would soon become the go-to-guy for other functions. He started to get involved in other regions as people valued his inputs. Amit was well read and well informed; he knew what was happening not only in his industry but also in those that were adjacent. He kept a tab on the latest trends in technology, consumer behaviour and innovation. He was on the fast track and within eighteen months he was promoted.

Amit had worked mostly with small teams; even in this latest position he had a team of only six analysts. Their skill sets and temperaments were similar to his, if not the same. His team loved him as he was non-interfering, yet he was always there to solve issues and help them whenever they got stuck. He was quite particular about striking the famous work-life balance and he encouraged that for his team as well. He worked hard and stayed focused while in the office so that he could leave on time, and that was why long coffee breaks and leisurely lunches were not his thing. He was very professional in his approach. He didn't indulge much in small talk and was always supportive of his team and his peers.

Twelve months before his conversation with Cindy, the company had gone through a major restructuring globally, which meant consolidation of a few functions and roles. All the leaders in the region were a little anxious and no one was sure which roles and functions would be impacted and by how much. The rumour mill was working overtime. Finally, at a town hall meeting, the CEO announced the new structure. Although the company had made significant efforts to minimize redundancies, quite a few leaders were impacted.

Over the next few days the new organization structure was announced, and Amit was part of the impacted party. He would no longer do his existing role, one of his team members would be elevated and she would take over. He was now the site leader, which meant that he was responsible for all the functions and people on that site—there were 2000 people! Amit hadn't done such a role before and was initially intimidated by the size and spread involved. He spoke to his supervisor and was assured of his full support and confidence in him. Amit also spoke to his mentor and some colleagues and they all told him that it was a great opportunity, and that he would manage it well.

He wasn't worried about the complexities of the role; what made Amit anxious was that some of his current peers would become his direct reports. Amit was a friendly person; he met his peers in the corridors every day and interacted with them in meetings, conferences and off-sites. But he did not have a lot of information on how they were personally. He wasn't sure how his peers would react to this new structure and him being their new boss.

The new structure was to come into effect after sixty days and that gave Amit time to think through his transition plan. He drew up a schedule of meetings with all the teams and his direct reports, and made a list of questions he wanted to ask them. He was very methodical in his approach and that was his strength. In those sixty days, Amit read all the reports and material available on the other functions and he got a fairly good understanding of what his new role would entail.

When the new structure came into force, Amit felt ready. He started with an all-hands meet. He felt it would be the perfect start for him to share his opinion about each department's performance. This turned out to be a mistake. He went on to share his views on the gaps at the overall site level. While Amit was being analytical and objective, the others didn't see it like that. His peers, who had been leading these functions, were definitely not happy, and Amit couldn't read the reactions clearly. He then held a string of meetings with each department. Amit asked a lot of questions, which the teams often didn't have the answers to. The next three to four months passed by quickly.

Amit was working hard, spending longer hours than usual in the office. He was too preoccupied to feel and observe the changes around him. His interaction with his peers had become even less. They did not ask him to join them for coffee, or post-work drinks, as they used to once.

Amit continuously checked in with his manager and was assured that he was on the right track and was doing fine. After a few months, he realized that his entire day was spent in and out of meetings and reviews. He started missing his old role in strategy. He felt he wasn't doing anything worthwhile. He didn't enjoy sitting in the meetings where, for hours, the new layout of the office was discussed, or the location of an off-site meeting was debated. It wasn't that he didn't think those were important matters, but he wasn't clear about the value he was adding. He knew the people in the room were experts and would make the right decision. He started to decline these meetings. People interpreted this as Amit's disinterest. Amit didn't communicate why he was declining the meetings as he assumed that his colleagues would understand his logic. That was how the gap started to widen.

Slowly, Amit discovered that his new role was not his cup of tea. He was starting to feel lonely. He felt a huge vacuum, but couldn't understand why. When he spoke with some of his direct reports, they told him all the right things but not necessarily what was on their minds. Amit could sense that something was brewing but couldn't put his finger on it. His logical mind ignored his instincts—that remains his biggest regret till today. He had made up his mind that he would do the role for another year and then move back to strategy, as running operations wasn't his thing.

After nine months in the role, the annual employee engagement survey was rolled out. Amit was slightly nervous about the result, but he was confident that people would appreciate his empowering hands-off style and the efficiency that he was driving to make their job easier. The results took him by surprise. While the overall site results were at the company's average, they were below the previous cycle and his own results were far below the mark. His direct reports had rated him poorly and that had brought down the overall results. Most of the comments said something to the effect of 'we don't know the real

Amit'. This perplexed him—he didn't understand what this meant. He wanted to speak with his team directly but thought that could be counterproductive.

He spent a week processing all the comments and reflecting on his style. He thought he would reach out to the head of HR, Cindy, and ask her to run a focus group with his team to get more details. But before he could do that, Cindy asked for a meeting with him.

The conversation with Cindy left him at a loss. The senior leadership had seen the results and they were displeased, to say the least. They wanted to know what actions he would be taking to improve the situation. Cindy shared that his promotion could be in jeopardy. As she was talking, he realized that very quickly he had gone from being the blue-eyed boy to being dropped like a hot potato. All of this was on the basis of a survey of the last nine months. He wanted to ask why all the work he had done in the last three years had not been taken into account. What about the expertise and knowledge that he brought to the table? What happened to all the talk about taking a risk? But he decided to keep quiet. He walked back to his office with a sense of betrayal.

He was already on the brink of getting into a leader's block due to the lack of excitement in the role and this incident acted as a catalyst.

Amit shared with me that the next eight weeks were tough. Even though he had to put up a brave front, internally he was in turmoil. He didn't know where to start, he found himself going into a shell and shutting down. His close friends and family saw the shift in his behaviour and temperament.

He took a one-week break and used that time to reflect. He thought about his strengths, his performance in the role, the things he probably could have done differently and why he had taken up the role in the first place. He could answer most of the questions but not necessarily with complete clarity. He needed some objectivity, so he reached out to one of his mentors who had experience in running large organizations. Amit said that the three-hour discussion with his mentor changed his outlook. He realized that he was using his old skill set to be successful in a totally new and different environment. What had worked for him as a strategy leader didn't work for him as an operations leader and he needed to change that.

Amit returned to work rejuvenated and charged up. He had clarity as to what he wanted to do and he went about doing it quickly. One of the first things he did was to meet his direct reports and share with them how he felt about the survey results. He then asked them if they would be willing to help him through some of the actions that would help him engage better with the teams. He spent time with each one of them individually to understand them professionally and personally, and also used this as an opportunity to share more about himself. Initially, he felt awkward sharing things about himself, but soon he started to enjoy it as he found many common interests with the team. He made changes to his approach, he became more inclusive, started indulging in regular coffee chats and the occasional leisurely lunch. He started to take more interest in people's overall well-being. As his mentor had explained, this was a people's business and he needed to change his operating style.

When I interviewed Amit, the next annual survey was about to be rolled out. I asked him if he was nervous and he said, 'I don't know the score, but I am confident that I have done the right things with the right intentions.' I asked him how he was feeling as he looked back. He told me that it had been a great learning process and journey. There had been many learnings, but three things stood out for him:

a. As a leader you can't rely only on one core skill set. You need to be multifaceted and build different leadership skills and styles. You can't be a one-trick pony.

b. You must harness the power of open communication. You may have the right intentions and you may care for people, but if they don't feel and see that care, then you are not communicating enough.

c. It is important to have mentors and advisers, and the humility to ask for help.

Even though I knew the answer, I asked him if his organization could have done more to support him. He smiled and answered, 'They could have been a little patient before dropping me like a hot potato.' I agree, his organization could have supported him as he was transitioning into the new role. He had stepped out of his comfort zone and he should have been appreciated for stepping up. For me, it was very encouraging to see Amit come out of leader's block with so much panache and positivity.

## The Promotion

Andrea was waiting for the month-end with mixed feelings. She was excited and nervous, though more nervous. She had been working for a large retail chain for eight years and had done well. She had joined as a store manager and through her people-centricity and ability to understand customers, she had climbed up the ladder quite fast, all within a six-year period. However, in the last two years she had started to feel a slowdown in her progress. She had been passed over for promotion a couple of times and the only feedback that she had received was that she was not prepared for it or she should wait a while as it would only be a matter of time before she was promoted.

Andrea was loved by the people in the business; people who had worked with her praised her nurturing nature. There were only two things that she cared about: her customers and her people. This was the recipe for her success and it had served her well so far. Her seniors acknowledged her strengths but also realized that in order to move to the next level she had to toughen up to make difficult decisions. In the past she had pushed back heavily on several occasions when it came to making changes. This was especially true when it had been regarding reducing costs or cutting down staff.

These instances had created the impression that she was uncooperative and not collaborative. It led her seniors to raise the question, was she ready for the next level? They felt that she lacked the ability to take a tough stand or have difficult conversations, and present the boldness of a leader. Her strengths that had served her so well were now holding her back. Andrea had never received this feedback directly from any of her seniors. It was a matrix organization where she had two managers, and neither of them had given her clear feedback in the last two years. Therefore, she continued to operate the way that had worked for her thus far.

Andrea's operating style was very inclusive. She lived by the mantra that she was in this business to serve the customer and she could do that successfully, but only if she took care of her people. She was aware about the business side of things, but it didn't excite her as much, and she didn't invest enough time to find out more. When she sat in management meetings she found herself disengaged. She couldn't relate to the discussions and arguments on budgets, future projections and cost constraints. She hadn't realized that this attitude would not take her far and could, in fact, work against her.

Finally, the promotions list came out and she wasn't promoted. She couldn't believe it. It was the second time in a row that she had missed out. This time the decision made her bitter. She couldn't understand what she had missed. The last time she had been told that it was just a matter of time, but no specific feedback had been given to her.

Andrea made up her mind to get that feedback. She tried to schedule time to meet with both her managers together, but due to their travel plans that didn't seem feasible. So she decided to speak with them separately. One of her managers, Vanessa, was relatively new, which didn't help Andrea because promotions at the senior level were a consensus-driven process. It was almost like campaigning for votes for your candidates in the elections.

In her conversation with Vanessa, Andrea was surprised to find out that William, her other manager, hadn't bothered to give much background about her to Vanessa. Vanessa wasn't even aware that Andrea had been passed over for a promotion the last time. This disturbed Andrea. Vanessa gave her vague feedback, such as she needed to explore more and develop some business acumen.

Andrea then had a call with William who had been her manager for the last eighteen months and had been with the company for a while. He knew Andrea fairly well. He told her that the leadership team knew she was an excellent person and they valued her skills and contributions, but they thought she was not ready for the next big role yet. Andrea wasn't satisfied with this and pushed to get some specifics. William shared that her reluctance to understand operations, especially the financials, and her avoidance of taking tough calls with her people were some of the things that were holding her back. He said that she needed to work on her visibility.

Andrea wasn't convinced as she thought she was doing a great job of managing her people and the customers. She thought that maybe she was not assertive enough in asking for a promotion or maybe she was not doing enough political networking or relationship building. She was a strong believer in meritocracy and thought that if there was something to be corrected then it was the evaluation system and not her. She was convinced that none of the feedback she had been given was genuine or correct.

The months that followed this conversation were among the most unproductive for Andrea. Though she was keeping up a brave front and doing what she was supposed to do, on the inside she had shut down. Her engagement levels had plummeted, she was becoming cynical, and she complained to everyone that she interacted with. Soon, others around her started to notice these changes. She had stopped putting her hand up for any new initiatives. She was experiencing leader's block.

This went on for about four to five months.

I asked her how she came out of it.

She smiled and said that it took a lot of courage and humility to tell herself that she was wrong— that maybe there was something she was missing and that she should give others the benefit of the doubt.

I complimented her as it does take a lot of maturity and self-awareness to not only think like that but also act on it.

Andrea went back to her managers, and this time, with an open mind. She took inputs from them to make a specific plan of action. She did a six-month rotation with the financial controller's group. She spent time understanding the back end of the business, financials and budgets. She started asking questions in meetings if she didn't understand something. She took every opportunity to be in front of the leadership team. She stretched herself and started to have the difficult conversations with people regarding their performance and behaviour.

In the next round she was promoted.

Andrea said that while her delayed promotion had pushed her into a block, it also gave her great learnings for her leadership journey. She told me something so profound in such a matter-of-fact way!

She told me that her first learning was to always have clear and direct conversations with her people. In her desire to be nice to people and not hurt them, she had evaded those conversations that were necessary for them to grow. She realized the negative impact this had when her own manager avoided giving her direct and specific feedback. She had got a taste of her own medicine.

As she looked back, Andrea admitted that her reaction to the rejection could have hurt her reputation and, in a way, confirmed to the leadership team that they had made the right decision by not promoting her. As a leader, one should be able to handle both positive and negative outcomes in a professional way.

Andrea looked at this as a growth and development opportunity, as she wasn't equipped to handle rejection. She realized that no business school or organization teaches you how to handle rejection. Such an important point! Often, leaders find it difficult to deal with rejections, mainly due to their past success, and when it does happen their reaction is typically negative.

Andrea now actively mentors and works with mid-level managers in her organization on how to handle rejections.

To me, Andrea's story highlights a few things apart from her maturity. Once again, the role of the organization (the manager) in communicating clearly to its leaders was the key. If Andrea's managers had been more direct with her she could have worked on the problems earlier and avoided the leader's block, which impacted not only her but also the organization. Many leaders that I interviewed had shared similar experiences around not being promoted. Most had expected that they would be and were very disappointed when they were not. The organization had been elusive about the reasons.

Since at the junior and mid-levels the promotions and growth come at a fast pace, leaders are not equipped to handle a slowdown or perceived rejection. Having been a business leader, I know that it is not only a leader's competence that drives a promotion decision. Other factors, including the requirements for a certain role, the budget and business needs also come into play. The gap is created when this is not explained clearly to the leader who is expecting the promotion.

The second factor that stood out for me was the importance of having a high level of self-awareness in leaders. Leaders sometime fall into a success trap. They continue to do what has brought them success to date. In the case of Andrea, her focus on customers and her team had brought her the initial success and she expected that alone would get her to the next level. She didn't do enough to expand her competence and skills. In her case she eventually recognized and acknowledged her block and worked to overcome it. For leaders, there is a certain amount of unlearning and relearning to be done at every level and they need to be prepared for that.

This case also clearly demonstrates how to turn an issue on its head; how to convert a challenge into an opportunity. Andrea not only came out of the leader's block with clarity, she decided to use it as a developmental opportunity for herself, and then decided to take that learning to others—especially emerging leaders. It gave her the perspective that so many around her could be going through something similar. She started to talk more openly in order to prepare leaders to face the situation when the results were not what they were expecting. She used her own case as an example to demonstrate the lesson, which was powerful.

Organizations don't do enough to encourage their leaders to talk about failures and setbacks. No leader wants to acknowledge these things. We need more leaders like Andrea who not only acknowledge their setbacks, but also use them to help emerging leaders. This will have a ripple effect and will help drive the culture of openness, not only in their department but also across the organization.

To me, the biggest takeaway from Andrea's story was the need for organizations to proactively prepare their leaders for failure and rejection.

## The Identity

Sameer, aka Sam, was excited when he signed his first contract. It had been a long journey for him to get there. The last five years had been a rollercoaster ride for him. He had gone from being a senior executive at a major oil and gas corporation to leading the deal for the sale of a family business to becoming an entrepreneur.

Sam had gone to the US for his master's degree and had stayed on to work there. He had joined an American multinational oil and gas corporation and went on to work for them for the next fifteen years. Sam was smart and sincere with a great sense of humour. He was quickly accepted in the leadership development programme and, as part of the programme, was rotated in different divisions of the business every six months. By the end of the two-year programme, Sam had become a well-known name amongst management. He had utilized the rotations to not only learn about the business, but also create a network within the leadership team and build visibility for himself. He went on to have a great career in the company and climbed the leadership ladder rapidly.

Sam's father was a well-known name in India. He was a successful entrepreneur and had built a large infrastructure company. After forty years in the business, he was heading towards retirement. A multinational infrastructure company was keen to buy him out. Sam's father thought it was a great opportunity, but he couldn't do the deal himself, he needed help.

Sam had always taken a keen interest in his father's business and had advised him on various occasions, but had never seen himself running it. When his father asked him if he could spearhead the deal for the sale of his company, Sam was in two minds. He was a little reluctant as this would mean relocating to India, at least for the short term. But he also saw it as a great opportunity to taste and test the entrepreneurial world. After some deliberation, he decided to move to India.

This was a big move for Sam as he had never worked in India though he visited his parents twice a year and spent a few weeks in his father's offices each time, so there was familiarity. Once he arrived, he dived into his father's business to get a better understanding of it. He was excited by the project. After all these years he was his own boss and he felt he owed this to his father for everything he had done for him. The latter had played a big role in his decision to come back to India.

Sam put in a lot of effort for the next nine months to see the transaction through. It was a challenging period as he had to make quite a few adjustments, both personally and professionally. He had to unlearn and then learn a different style of working. The processes and systems weren't as sophisticated, the people were different and the culture was quite bureaucratic. He worked through these challenges as he knew it was temporary, though not without frustration.

After the company was sold, Sam was again in two minds about whether he should go back to the US or stay in India. His experience with freedom and entrepreneurship had been a very good one, and he wanted to explore a few options. His family wasn't ready to stay on in India, so they moved back to the US while he remained in India and promised to visit them every month.

The next few months were very stimulating for Sam. He met a lot of people, had great conversations, explored different sectors and finally identified the area where he wanted to invest. His expertise was in the energy sector—oil and gas, power and associated technology—and he wanted to work in the renewable energy space. He set up a small team. The timing was right. Sam and his team aggressively started the sales process. Once they won their first few projects, Sam moved back to the US but continued to travel back and forth. He hired a competent team to run the company. The next two to three years were very productive. They got a few major projects under their belt, the pipeline looked healthy and the momentum was perfect for the business to take off.

Then there was an unexpected change in the market—the commodities market crashed! Oil prices went down and renewable energy was no longer as attractive to investors.

This had a huge impact on Sam's business and disrupted their future plans and projections. Their customers became sceptical and a lot of decisions were stalled, though luckily they continued to work on current projects. Sam's trips to India were more frequent and for longer durations. He made every effort to salvage the situation and bring the company back on track. He soon realized that if he had to scale up and sustain the business in India, he would have to stay there for longer. The remote working model wasn't a feasible option in the long run. The situation once again presented him with a difficult choice.

After nine excruciating months, Sam called it quits.

As Sam shared his story with me, I saw the part about his involvement with his father's company as the first step in his own entrepreneurial journey. But I was wrong; Sam had told me that story to highlight the dilemma of making personal choices. He had left a promising career to help his father and then left an emerging business to be with his family.

As leaders we don't think often and enough about the personal factors that impact us.

The months leading up to the decision to shut down his business were painful. He had made the bold decision to quit his job at the peak of his career—he found himself questioning that move! At times he found himself doubting his own capabilities. His father had built and run a successful business for forty years and he couldn't take his beyond three years. He was filled with self-doubt and his confidence hit an all-time low. He found himself becoming irritable, short-tempered and volatile, and his sense of humour also deserted him. These were all symptoms of leader's block.

I asked Sam what was the toughest part during this period. He said it was the identity crisis he suffered. He said that for the longest time his identity had been tied to the organization he worked for. His business card defined who he was, he enjoyed a lot of privileges, perks and attention thanks to it. It was only when he quit and didn't have the fancy business card that he realized he had no identity. For example, earlier, when he went to networking events, he would hand out his business card and gain almost immediate attention from those he gave it to. Conversations were easy to start. But without that card, things were different. He would spend five minutes explaining what he did and a lot of times the disinterest of his listeners was obvious.

This resonated with me as I meet so many leaders across different organizations and the majority of them define themselves by their titles or designations. In fact, in my workshops, when I ask participants to introduce themselves, they always start with their titles and designations. Sam's story made me wonder what would happen if the titles and designations of these leaders were taken away.

Coming back to Sam, I wanted to know what he did next. Sam said that once he had made the decision to quit his India venture, he wasn't sure if he wanted to go back to the corporate world or continue his entrepreneurial adventure. He took a few months off and used that time to reflect. As he stepped back he realized that there had been a lot of learning for him in the last four years. His involvement in his father's business had given him a glimpse of what it took to build and sustain a large business. He called his India venture an 'elegant failure' that taught him a lot about entrepreneurship. He reached out to a few of his mentors and close friends and discussed his next steps with them.

He began to focus on getting back into his zone of positivity and possibilities. He started playing tennis at the club again and joined a meditation group. He started going out with his friends and found his sense of humour returning. His family supported him through this time.

After about three months of deliberation, Sam decided to start a new venture in the US. When I met him, his business was twelve months old and was looking good!

I asked him if there was one specific learning that he had taken from the whole experience. He said that he was lucky that he had got the chance to recreate his identity and that this time it didn't represent what he did, but who he was. He was glad that he had had these experiences as they had made him mentally stronger and given him a lot of clarity about the future, his capabilities and the opportunities ahead. They had also taught him to step back and reflect.

For me, Sam's story highlights a few interesting points. The first is the point about personal and external factors impacting our lives. As leaders we need to acknowledge that there will always be things that are beyond our control. Logic, analytical thinking, reasoning and business acumen are not the only things that drive our decision-making; personal and external factors play a big role too.

Second is the point that Sam raised about identity. This is a deeper issue that many leaders struggle with, especially as they become more senior. I believe that every leader should revisit their identity regularly to see if it truly reflects who they are. In general, we tend to link our identity with the definition of success as described by others. When we gather the courage and confidence to define our own measurement or metric of success, we are truly liberated, and we create the identity that we want. This point struck a chord with me. I experienced the pain of an identity crisis and the challenges of recreating my identity when I quit my corporate career after twenty years and started a leadership consulting firm.

Thirdly, I appreciated the maturity with which Sam handled the situation. He weighed all the pros and cons, evaluated the impact of his decisions on his family and then made the decision. He showed a lot of thoughtfulness and put his loved ones ahead of his ambitions. I am sure this will serve him very well. As the saying goes, charity starts at home. This is the strong leadership trait that we often miss out—the human side—looking beyond our own needs and desires.

Last, but not the least, is the importance of stepping back and reflecting. I could almost feel the chaos and the predicament as Sam's story was unfolding. It was hard to imagine how Sam kept his sanity through this time. The power of reflection yet again wins. It is an underrated practice, as we are always looking for more productivity, faster results and immediate solutions. There is so much merit in taking time off to reflect, look at the bigger picture and consciously create the future that we want. This also helps to build resilience. So, the next time we get blocked we are better prepared to face it and overcome it. Sam's experience has helped him build resilience and prepare for future setbacks if and when they happen.

This story shows the human side of the leader; what happens behind the scenes that is not visible to people. We don't get to see this very often, and I am grateful to Sam for sharing it with you and me.

Taking a cue from GE's former CEO Jack Welch's famous quote, 'control your destiny or someone else will', I would say, create your identity or someone else will!

## The Divorce

Jonathan had worked with one of the world's largest technology companies for twenty-five years. It was technically his first job after eighteen months of internship at a local service company. He took pride in being associated with the company. It had been his learning ground, or playground as he called it. He had learnt everything about technology and leadership from his seniors in the company. He was grateful for everything the organization had offered him in those years. Jonathan was a hard-working employee, he never shied away from going the extra mile to serve the company. He was a good-natured person, always willing to help others. He wore his love for the company on his sleeve and would never say anything against the company or the leadership, even jokingly. He strongly believed and lived by the organization's values, in fact he was values personified. He would never do anything that would jeopardize those values, for him they were sacrosanct, just like one's marriage vows!

It was the perfect marriage, as his friends would say in jest.

During his tenure in the company, Jonathan got the opportunity to work in different parts of the world, which he thoroughly enjoyed. Sometimes he did not like the location, but he accepted the assignment nonetheless. He believed someone had to do the job, and he was willing to be that someone for the company. In almost all cases, he put the company before himself.

Nobody thought that this would ever change.

Jonathan returned to his home base in the United Kingdom (UK) after being in different locations in Asia for ten years. He wanted to stay in the UK as his family didn't want to move around any more. He had applied for a job within the company and was confident that he would get it. Unfortunately, he didn't and the company hired an external candidate. He applied for another role, which wasn't his first choice, but as it was in the UK, he was fine with it. He didn't get that role either.

Jonathan had been away from the UK office for many years and there had been a lot of changes in the leadership team. He didn't know most of the people in the office and the vibe there was different. People were younger, a little less friendly and didn't speak to each other much. This was a huge change from what it used to be like and Jonathan knew it would take him some time to adjust. What he wasn't ready for was the aggressive leadership style that had become pervasive in the office. People spoke over each other, spoke behind each other's backs and didn't always tell the truth or keep their word. This was a big shift for him.

Jonathan spoke to a few of his erstwhile colleagues and they suggested that he should speak to some senior leaders. He fixed a meeting with one of them.

The conversation with this leader didn't go very well. He told Jonathan that he wasn't fit for the roles he had applied for. Jonathan didn't quite understand what that meant. His senior asked him to apply for another role. Jonathan was appalled as that role was a level below his current designation. He wasn't willing to step down. Jonathan reached out to some of the leaders he knew in that region and they all told him the same thing in different ways—that he should take whatever he was getting as there weren't too many options for him. Jonathan was taken aback; he couldn't believe this was happening to him.

He discussed the situation with his family, weighed his options and decided to take on the role that was available to him. The thought of leaving the company didn't even occur to him. He decided to put aside the negativity and approached his new role with positivity and gusto. His new manager was quite young and had been with the company for a little over four years. In the initial months, Jonathan managed to keep his positivity and did his job with sincerity. He accepted his manager's input with the right spirit even though he sometimes didn't agree. Jonathan continued to work but was miserable on the inside. He wasn't enjoying the work he was doing, he felt stifled as his way of working was very different from his manager's style. He couldn't understand his manager and never seemed to meet his requirements and expectations. His self-respect, self-esteem, self-confidence, everything, was negatively impacted. His unhappiness started to show in his demeanour, he wasn't himself at work and that continued at home. Jonathan was experiencing a leader's block. What hurt him the most was the fact that his company could treat him in such a manner.

Jonathan's family and close friends became worried about him. They advised him to look for opportunities outside his organization. His reaction was always a vehement no, but that was about to change. One day, after an altercation with his manager, Jonathan realized that it was time for a divorce.

As Jonathan narrated this to me, I couldn't believe he was the same person. The Jonathan I was meeting was a confident, charming and dynamic leader—a far cry from the Jonathan he had described. Jonathan was now the CIO of a midsize software company and the company was going places.

I asked Jonathan what had made him finally take the call to quit his previous role. In fact, why had he delayed the decision? Jonathan explained that he had wanted to give the marriage a fair chance. Like most marriages, he felt it was just a temporary phase, but soon he realized that staying in an unhappy marriage is bad for both parties. So he thought the best thing would be to part ways. He said that it was not an easy decision as he had spent his prime years with that company.

I asked Jonathan, now that he had moved on and had the objectivity to look back, what had happened? How did he come to find himself in a situation like that? He said that in all honesty it was he who had probably been at fault. He hadn't kept pace with the changes and had probably taken the company for granted as much as the company had taken him for granted. In the ten years that he was in Asia, the company had changed dramatically to keep up with the changes in the industry and the business environment. The traditional roles no longer existed and the skill sets, competencies and mindset required to do the new roles were very different. He probably hadn't felt the impact of these changes much sitting in the smaller markets.

I asked him if he had kept in touch with his network when he had moved to different markets, and he said he was guilty of not doing that. In hindsight, he acknowledged that it was one of the biggest mistakes he had made.

I admired Jonathan for being so forthcoming and honest with his story. There are many golden nuggets of learning within it.

As I reflected on Jonathan's story, a few things stood out for me. This is a scenario that a lot of expatriate leaders can relate to. Going back to your home country after being out for many years comes with its own set of challenges. One of the ways to mitigate those challenges is to keep your network active. Keeping in touch with your network is very important: the sponsors, the mentors, the peers, all play a big role in your growth and journey. We underestimate the power of networking and in Jonathan's case, if he had kept in touch with his network in the UK, his transition could have been smoother. He could have leveraged his network to look for a role even before he went back. He could have gained a better understanding of the dynamics in the office. Recently, somebody told me that networking is a new competency and it is called 'corporate savviness'.

Another thing that struck me was the importance of up-skilling, irrespective of your level. What worked for you yesterday may not serve you tomorrow. The workforce today is multigenerational and therefore there are bound to be conflicts and frictions. Leaders need to have the flexibility and adaptability to deal with this scenario. Working for younger managers or managers with different styles is a reality rather than an exception in today's world. It is a huge shift for leaders who have spent many years in a more traditional set-up.

Jonathan's action of calling it quits was wise. Sometimes the best decision is to make changes, whether within yourself or in your situation. He knew he had to take charge of the situation; he couldn't wait for the company to salvage it. As always, change is never easy, and for him it was particularly painful as he felt he was betraying his company by leaving it. But he had to bite the bullet eventually, which was good for both of them.

Jonathan's story highlights a critical, current and relevant trend—the culture transition in large and older organizations. The transition from being a more traditional organization to being a New Age organization. It's a fine balance. While organizations are responding to change and reinventing themselves, there is a high risk of jeopardizing their values if the transition is not navigated properly. The balance between old and new has to be struck delicately by its leaders. There is still a lot of merit in having experience on your side. While the young bring the ideas, the innovation and the fresh blood, an organization needs stability and experience to drive the execution. Similarly, there is a need to value employees who are loyal and have proven themselves over the years. The long-term employees help preserve the values and the ethos of the organization while new employees bring in objectivity and challenge the status quo.

Lastly, once again the importance of having open communication is highlighted. If Jonathan's senior had given him clear feedback, it would have been very helpful for him. The lack of communication about his role in the company not only impacted him, but also the organization. The impact of the immediate manager on the employee was another factor in this case. Jonathan was a seasoned leader, but even then his manager's attitude and behaviour impacted him immensely. No one is immune to this and therefore the onus is on the managers to be more open and transparent. They are responsible for their teams and their well-being. Jonathan's manager could have been more supportive of him and leveraged his experience in the company instead of sidelining him and micromanaging. It was clearly a missed opportunity.

I was impressed by Jonathan's spirit and ability to bounce back with vigour. He had reinvented himself and made himself relevant again. He didn't let his negativity impact him for too long. He recognized the block, acknowledged it and then worked to overcome it. He was quick to respond to the changing times and applied the learnings of his previous organization in his new job. He continued to leverage his years of experience while tweaking his style to meet the demands of today. In his new avatar as Jonathan 2.0, he truly embodies the essence of an agile leader!

During my conversation with Jonathan, not once did he bad-mouth his previous organization, and that speaks volumes about him.

## The Change

Lisa's promotion was announced. It was her second promotion since joining the company three years earlier. Her team had organized an impromptu celebration with cake and flowers. She was one of the shining stars of a fast-growing start-up. As she drove home that evening to share the news with her family, she realized she wasn't happy. She had a sense of guilt, she felt she didn't deserve the promotion.

Lisa had joined the start-up when it was at an inflection point. It had received its second round of funding and was getting ready for aggressive scaling up. She had come on board as part of the product team that worked closely with the CEO's office. Lisa had fifteen years of work experience with multiple consulting firms. She had a good track record, was hard-working, diligent and bright. She had been hired in the start-up by one of her ex-bosses. In fact, when he had approached her, she had initially been sceptical. Lisa had heard a lot about the negative environment of the start-up world, the crazy work hours, the pressure, the aggressive sales targets and the cut-throat competition. But the role attracted her; it sounded challenging and after a bit of convincing from her ex-boss she was on board.

It did take Lisa some time to adjust to the culture of the company. She came from a world where everything was structured, the roles were well defined, the deliverables were clearly laid out and the protocols for interacting with clients were clear. The focus on ethics and compliance was unparalleled, employees took a conservative approach if they were ever in doubt. Here, it was just the opposite. There was no structure, there were no protocols and no specific roles, and the only focus was growth and revenue. Everything else came after that.

To adjust and adapt to the new environment, Lisa had to change many things, from her operating style to her communication style; from how she wrote emails to even how she dressed, as business suits were a misfit in the new environment. She had to unlearn and relearn, but she was ready for the challenge. The company had some very experienced and smart people on the leadership team and she was excited to work with them.

Lisa settled in fast. There was no induction plan for her so she had to learn the ropes while on the job. She enjoyed the adrenaline rush of treading in unchartered waters, of working through the ambiguity to create a product from scratch and to completely own it. She worked an average of sixty to seventy hours a week, including the weekends. The leadership loved her dedication and the energy she brought to the table. One year passed in a jiffy. She got her first promotion after eighteen months in the role, with a handsome increment and some equity in the organization.

During the year prior to her second promotion, Lisa was so singularly focused on her work that she didn't notice the culture or vibes in the office.

After her promotion, Lisa got a seat at the leadership table. She was now part of the CEO's team and got to see the leaders up close. That was when she started getting exposed to the real work culture and ethics. The tone from the top was clear wherein the leadership team had chosen to give full autonomy to its managers without much supervision. With the objectives of growth and revenue, they had left the teams to figure out the 'how'. While this was empowering, it also encouraged internal competition which, if left unchecked, could become unhealthy.

This autonomous model was manageable initially as the company was small and the leaders knew most of the managers personally. But problems arose when the organization started to grow and hire more and more people. The new staff didn't know the background and for them, the company's culture was clear—get results at any cost!

Lisa saw this behaviour in her team too and tried to correct it. It didn't go well as every message from the top was directly or indirectly encouraging that behaviour. People were getting promoted and gaining increments purely on the basis of their results. How they achieved them was never questioned. This encouraged unscrupulous practices within teams. People got away with this because there weren't any strong compliance policies in place. Even if a few complaints of malpractice did come to the attention of the leadership team, they were taken lightly and ignored.

This started to bother Lisa. She talked to some of the people in her network and they all told her that that was the start-up culture and perhaps she was being too judgmental. She spoke to her CEO and he assured her that they would start focusing on the structure, culture and policies once they achieved the growth they had committed to the investors. She believed him and hoped that he would keep his word.

The company continued its fantastic growth trajectory. They were expanding in different regions, which meant hiring more people almost every day. With the expansion came the challenges that the leadership team had overlooked all this time. Lisa, while busy with her job, was very perceptive to the environment in the organization. As she walked around the office and visited other regions she saw that things weren't great, there was an underlying aggression in people—they tried to be better than their peers, and sometimes even supervisors.

Every time Lisa shared her concerns with the leadership team they brushed them aside. She heard the same thing—let's focus on growth, we will deal with this later.

Lisa began to get frustrated and struggled to focus. She started questioning her own work ethic. At the same time she wasn't sure if she was overreacting. She started to become disengaged. She began to question everything that was said and discussed in meetings. She started doubting the intention of every interaction with the leadership team. In fact, on occasion she found herself being loud and aggressive, which wasn't her style. She was getting into a leader's block.

Lisa spent the next three months in this quagmire, unsure of what do to. Her heart was no longer in her job. But she didn't want to make any hasty decisions that she would regret later. She really did believe in the mission and vision of the company and its founders. She decided to take a few weeks off. Everyone was surprised as it was a critical time for the company. The leadership team sensed that something was wrong. They knew that they couldn't afford to lose her at this crucial juncture.

Lisa took the time off to get clarity, to step back and reflect on the three years she had spent with the company and also to think about her future. When she came back, her promotion was announced. The next day she went up to the CEO and asked him if she could hire an executive coach and that was when Lisa contacted me.

She shared with me the details of her three years in the company. She told me how they had been the most challenging and productive years of her career. She hadn't enjoyed the same degree of autonomy, empowerment, freedom and creativity in any of her previous jobs, but she didn't like the culture that was slowly emerging in the organization. That bothered her. Her dilemma was whether to continue or to quit.

I asked her if the other seven leaders in the executive team felt that way too, but she wasn't sure. Over the course of the next four to six weeks, Lisa met with all the executive members of the team, one-on-one. To her surprise, most of them shared her concerns, but said that they didn't have the time and bandwidth to do anything about it. There were two leaders who didn't agree with Lisa's concerns. Lisa updated the CEO about her conversations and requested him to step in.

The CEO was a smart man. He asked Lisa, along with the head of HR, to put together a plan for changing the culture of organization. This initiative was initially resisted by the same two outspoken leaders, but the supporters outnumbered them.

Over the next couple of months, Lisa worked with the head of HR to put together the organization's new culture norms and redefine the company values. They changed the performance management system so that people were evaluated not only on the numbers but also on the 'how'. These changes were communicated by the CEO through focus groups and employee meetings. Within a few months, the results started to show.

By the end of our engagement, Lisa had successfully led the change in the culture of the organization without changing its spirit. Out of the two outspoken leaders, one was fired for an integrity issue and other one changed sides. In our last session Lisa said, 'Ritu, thanks for helping me find my purpose.'

For Lisa, this became the turning point of her career and life. She saw the impact she could make being in the position of power and influence. She continued to head the product team along with championing the changes in the organization and over the following nine months, the HR team was ramped up. Processes and policies were put in place to drive the culture of collaboration. The focus on growth and revenue continued along with a focus on people and culture.

Lisa has been with the company for seven years now and is still going strong.

I am very proud of Lisa. She had the easier option of quitting and moving on to another organization, but she decided to stay and lead the change. She personified the saying 'be the change you want to see in the world' in her own way. She made this her purpose. She genuinely cared for the company and its people and therefore decided to do something about the problems she saw within it. She recognized her leader's block and decided to address it. She reached out for help.

For me, Lisa's case highlighted a few things. It is very easy to become part of a culture, even if you don't like it. It takes a lot of courage to stick your neck out and call out something that you don't agree with or like. Secondly, leaders are responsible for setting the tone of the organization. If that is not done with care, or is ignored, it can impact the organization negatively and drive away the best of people. In this case, the executive team didn't necessarily have the wrong intentions, but it didn't give the culture of the organization much importance. It undermined the value of setting the correct culture right from the start. Lastly, even one or two leaders can impact the whole organization, especially in its early days.

Even though this case is of a start-up, the learnings can be applied to a stable organization as well. The role of a leader, whether of a team, department, region or company, comes with a lot of responsibility. People are watching leaders all the time. Sometimes their silence can be taken as an endorsement, which is detrimental to the health of the organization.

The credit also goes to the CEO. While he was more focused on growth and overlooked Lisa's concerns, he kept an open mind. He recognized and acknowledged the situation and its seriousness. He realized Lisa's potential and capability and knew she would be the best person to drive a change. He appreciated her commitment to the company and didn't shy away from rewarding her appropriately. Organizations need more leaders like Lisa and they need to celebrate them more.

## The Mistake

It was one of the toughest conversations that Philip had had in his entire twenty-year career. Before the meeting, he tried to remember the best practices of preparing for a difficult conversation that he had learnt in a workshop sometime back. He had been dreading this confrontation, but he knew that he had put it off for too long and that it was overdue.

Philip was a senior leader with experience in several multinational companies. He had been with his current organization for the last seven years. Three years back he had been asked to head a new division. As part of that he had to hire a new team. Philip was well versed with the hiring process and in fact was a very good judge of people. He had always managed to recruit not only the most competent people but also the perfect fits for the roles. The hiring team relied heavily on his input and his peers would often request him to sit on the interview panel for their hiring. He had hired hundreds, if not thousands, of people during the course of his career.

Before an interview, Philip would go through the candidate's resumé thoroughly to look for stability and consistency. His sharp eyes would pick up any anomalies. During the interview itself, his style was quite the opposite, he asked very few questions. His questions were not directly related to the job or the role. He liked to understand the people, their temperaments, their outlook and their attitude rather than just their competence. Philip would decide within the first five minutes if he was going to hire the person or not. It was an instinctive and gut-driven decision rather than a purely data-driven one. Once he shortlisted a candidate he would ask the HR team to do the necessary reference checks.

Philip had hired four people out of the five he needed on his team. He was looking out for one more. His search stopped when he got an email from Ning. He had known Ning for about six years, though she had never worked with him. Ning was a senior member in the team that was led by Philip's close friend in the organization he had worked in previously. She was a smart woman with great communication skills. She had a pleasing personality and was a go-getter. Philip was surprised to receive her email. He thought she was doing well in her current job. She told him that she was looking to expand her expertise and the role on his team would give her that opportunity.

Since Philip knew her, he expedited the hiring process. The interview was quickly set up and within a few weeks Ning was on board. Philip's team was complete.

For the first few months everyone was busy with orientation and settling into their new roles and the new division. Philip was proud of his team; each of them had different skill sets and personalities, and there was true diversity at all levels. The team got along well. After about six months, Philip started to see some friction in the team meetings; the humour and open conversations were missing. People spoke only about their project updates. He let it pass thinking that it was the pressure of the work. But soon Philip realized that he was wrong in ignoring it.

In team meetings he tried to ask the team what was wrong. When he didn't get any specific feedback, he decided to talk to his team members, one-on-one. Those conversations left him confused. While he got similar inputs from four of the team members, the story from Ning was very different. He decided to collect more data by talking to multiple stakeholders. Through the next few weeks he had heard enough anecdotes.

Ning had been a good performer, she met her targets and metrics, she managed her stakeholders very well, but she wasn't a team player. The team felt that she put herself before it. Teamwork was key to Philip as their department was new and their roles were not very well defined. Their goals and objectives were interlinked with each other's performances. The team felt that Ning always took the credit for the work being done by the others in the team. She projected that she was doing all the heavy lifting, and the team wasn't happy about this.

Philip had an open conversation with Ning and he gave her the feedback he had gathered. She didn't agree with him, but gave him a patient hearing. He thought that she would work on the input she had received and wanted to give her some time to do so.

Philip watched her closely for the next few months. On the face of it, Ning was the friendliest person around. It was difficult to find anything wrong with her performance, she was good at impression management, but she seemed to be creating a lot of unrest in the team. Philip didn't take any action. It was only when his team came to him and openly said that they could not work with Ning did he realize the enormity of the situation.

When Philip spoke to his friend from his previous company, he found out that Ning was a good individual contributor but not necessarily a team player. He looked at her resumé again and wondered how he could have missed such an obvious point. He had made the mistake of hiring Ning in a hurry. She had not stayed in any company for more than twelve to eighteen months. Since he had felt he knew Ning, he hadn't even asked her 'his' questions. He had shortchanged his own process!

He knew the conversation with Ning wouldn't be easy, but it had to be done. He had decided to move her out of the team.

I was a little surprised when Philip shared this reason for his leader's block. I hadn't heard this from any leader before, but I clearly saw his point after listening to his whole story.

Philip couldn't believe that he had made a mistake. He had been swayed by his unconscious bias, which had made him hire Ning in haste. He hadn't done all the checks and due diligence that he normally would. He hadn't even bothered to check with his friend who had worked with her. How could he have missed following his own process? Philip called this his leadership failure.

After Philip first heard about Ning's attitude from his team, he didn't take any action. It took him almost six months to make the decision to move her out. He said that during that time, he felt that parts of his leadership attributes were blocked. While he knew something was wrong, he didn't do enough to get into the details. He overlooked the vibes in the team meetings and interactions. He didn't want to acknowledge that he had made a mistake as it wasn't easy to do that. He didn't want to look bad. In hindsight, he felt that he didn't do justice to his team. They had expected him to listen and act on their concerns. He had created a trust barrier, which would take a long time to overcome.

Even after Philip realized that he had made a hiring mistake, it took him a while to accept it and that duration of denial caused him to get into a leader's block. His self-confidence was impacted as he had failed in an area that he took pride in. Actually, the seemingly small things can cause a lot of anxiety and unrest within leaders as they have a reputation and image to guard.

Leaders are always under pressure to be right and that's why it is not easy for them to accept their mistakes. It takes courage to not only accept a mistake but also to act. I appreciated Philip's honesty. I asked him what had prompted him to finally take the decision to speak to Ning. He said that he felt dishonest as he wasn't setting a good example for his team. He wasn't walking the talk and that made him restless.

Philip's story gives us a glimpse of the day-to-day challenges that leaders go through that are not very visible or may not be obvious. Generally, leaders get blocked when they face challenges or obstacles that are created by someone else; either the organization, environment or the people around them. After listening to Philip, I realized that sometimes a leader's own actions or inactions can get them into a block. I am sure a lot of leaders will be able to relate to this scenario.

My biggest takeaway from this story was that sometimes the outwardly small things can lead to leader's block if not attended to or if left unchecked. Organizations could help ease that pressure by creating an environment where leaders feel supported when they make mistakes. Also, building self-awareness is a skill that is becoming critical for leaders to thrive in today's world.

## Summary

Leader's block is the new normal. As leaders you are not super human beings. You are humans who have attained a leadership position due to your hard work, effort and experience. Like all humans, you are prone to failures, obstacles, challenges and blocks. I have termed these challenges and obstacles as leader's block. This is the phase when leaders are not able to perform to the best of their abilities.

The impact of leader's block is felt not only by you as a leader but also by those around you—your teams, your families and your organization. There are tangible impacts such as attrition and cost of unproductivity, as well as intangible impacts such as burnout, derailment and loss of morale. Leader's block thus cannot be ignored or overlooked!

The triggers for leader's block are wide-ranging, from being systemic, to situational, to personal. They are unique to each leader with common themes and patterns.

There are three key steps to overcome this phase.

a. **Recognize:** Learn to identify the symptoms. Observe the patterns of behaviour, emotions, thoughts and actions that are a deviation from your normal self. For example, are you quieter than usual, or do you find yourself disengaged in important meetings, or do you not enjoy what you are doing? Look out for telltale signs.

b. **Acknowledge:** Don't ignore these signs. Learn to accept that it is not possible to be performing at your best all the time. It is okay to say, 'I don't know', or 'I am stuck' or 'I need help'. No one can do it all by themselves. Organizations play an important role here. They need to support leaders by removing the taboo and stigma attached to asking for help. Organizations should create an environment and culture that encourages leaders to have open conversations about their challenges and setbacks, and also prepares emerging leaders for the road ahead.

c. **Overcome:** Based on your personality and situation, as well as the intensity of and trigger for leader's block, you could use one or more of these solutions:

i. B: Look at the BIG PICTURE.
ii. L: Sometimes, let things take their own course, LET IT PASS.
iii. O: Regularly seek the OPINIONS of those around you.
iv. C: Don't be afraid of CHANGING LANES when required.

   v.   K: Leverage KINSHIP to guide you and support you.

This book illustrates these points through the narratives and stories of leaders whom I have interviewed and coached. These are leaders who went through this phase and came out of it stronger, wiser and more resilient.

There are practices, rituals and habits that can help reduce the frequency and the intensity of leader's block. Build these practices into your routines to build resilience and be more effective and efficient as a leader and as a person:

a. Make time for reflection religiously.
b. Take time off and find some recreational activities outside work.
c. Be willing to unlearn and learn new ways of doing things.
d. Reach out for proactive feedback.

Finally, here is a checklist for you to monitor yourself and to build immunity:

a. Are you keeping aside some time to reflect daily?
b. Are you proactively collecting inputs from people who matter?

c. Do you work on the inputs that you collect?
d. Are you pursuing a hobby or vocation?
e. Are you doing something to constantly learn?
f. Do you have an activity that gets you into the flow?
g. Do you recognize your emotional triggers, what is causing them and their impact?
h. Do you clearly know your 'why'?
i. Is anything holding you back from making changes in your behaviour?
j. Do you have the key people in your ecosystem to support you?

If your answer is 'no' to more than five questions, you have work to do!

Leader's block is a phenomenon that can be applied to any field, be it sports, performance, arts, politics and even speaking. In April 2018, I spoke at the Asia Professional Speaker's Annual convention, which is part of Global Speaker's Federation, addressing an audience of 300 professional speakers from twenty-five countries. My topic was 'Speaker's Block', the triggers, the symptoms and the ways to overcome it. The topic resonated very well with the audience and I received great feedback.

To know more about the topic and its application to you, your team(s) and your organization, you can visit my website www.ritumehrish.com.

# Acknowledgements

I want to thank my husband, Gagan, for his tremendous patience and brutal feedback, and my children, Samar and Nandini, for being my biggest cheerleaders.

As they say, it takes a village to raise a child. The same applies to writing a book. There are many people who contributed to this book, starting with the leaders who agreed to do an interview with me, poured their hearts out with honesty and whose stories have made the book come alive.

I want to acknowledge my editor, Lohit Jagwani, for giving the book the final touches, Ocean Reeve, my book coach, who worked tirelessly with me over the last ten months.

Last, but not the least, my mentor, Fredrik Haren, who not only inspired me to write the book but also helped me coin the term 'leader's block'.